TIM CHAFFEY
GENERAL EDITORS
LAURA WELCH

Inside Noah's Ark

WHY IT WORKED

First printing: December 2016
Fourth printing: July 2017

Master Books®, P.O. Box 726, Green Forest, AR 72638

Master Books® is a division of
the New Leaf Publishing Group, Inc.

ISBN: 978-0-89051-932-5
ISBN: 978-1-61458-040-9 (digital)

Library of Congress Number: 2016948390

Cover and interior design by: Diana Bogardus

Cover Illustration by: Allen Greene

Please consider requesting that a copy of this volume be purchased by your local library system.

Printed in China

Please visit our website for other great titles:
www.masterbooks.com

For information regarding author interviews, please contact the publicity department at (870) 438-5288.

Master Books®
A Division of New Leaf Publishing Group
www.masterbooks.com

Table of Contents

Introduction

So the LORD said, "I will destroy man whom I have created from the face of the earth, both man and beast, creeping thing and birds of the air, for I am sorry that I have made them." But Noah found grace in the eyes of the LORD.

— Genesis 6:7–8

Noah's Ark has intrigued people for thousands of years. There are just so many questions related to this small collection of verses in the Book of Genesis. Has it been found? How did it work? Was it a real boat or just a religious metaphor? Could all the animals fit? Eight people, one boat, and the epic journey that saved representatives of the animal kinds — it is a biblical account that demands attention.

Hundreds of flood legends from around the world seem to echo the Genesis account. Early historians like Alexander Polyhistor and Josephus cited Berosus of Chaldea in describing the Ark being in a specific location that was visited by people who took small pieces of it with them to ward off evil. Over time, this view began to change, though many additional historical accounts continued to present it as reality rather than a morality tale.

Then as people began to see the Bible as less historical and more metaphorical, there began to be questions about the feasibility of Noah's Ark and whether the Great Flood could have even occurred. As people discounted the biblical timeline for a secular one that includes billions of years, the Ark became little more than a fairy tale. Even many believers unwittingly support such a view when they portray the Ark as looking more like a cute overstuffed bathtub. Secularists tried to make it appear that the boat, the Flood, and the whole account were impossibilities.

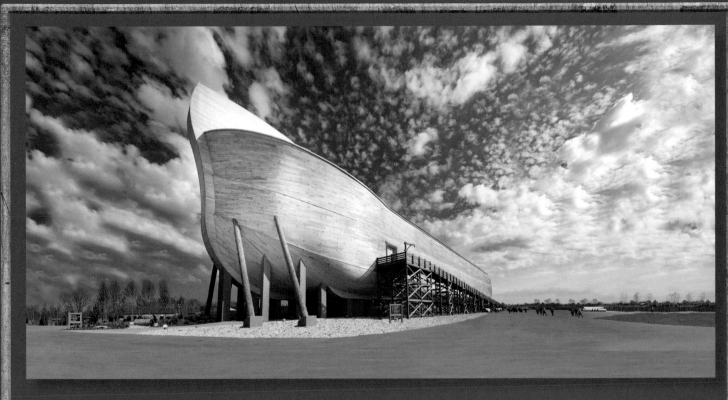

People's interest in Noah's Ark has not faded away — even in our modern and skeptical time. In a January 2010 poll by CBS News and Vanity Fair, Noah's Ark was the top choice for "which lost artifact would you most like to find," at 43 percent of all poll participants and 65 percent of those who identify as evangelicals.[1]

Now, at the Ark Encounter in Williamstown, Kentucky, a huge wooden replica of Noah's Ark has taken shape and confronts the skeptics with scientific details and other teaching that highlight the vessel and the Genesis account as viable history as they answer some of the world's most common and critical questions.

Why is this such an important effort? It is vital as a tool to show that God's Word about the history of God's world is true. If Noah was real, and the Ark was built, and the Flood occurred, what message is there for the world today?

The truth impacts our view of history from the very beginning — when man was created perfect and without sin. After mankind's Fall, the Bible tells us that by Noah's time, the world consisted of people whose only thoughts were of evil all the time. The only exception was Noah — who God would task to save part of His creation when His judgment was unleashed on the world.

This truth also affects our view of our origins. Ancient man was not the primitive ape-like creature that is so popularly depicted today. We see remarkable advances in the earliest civilizations that reveal lost and sophisticated knowledge of the world and the universe that has had to be "re-discovered."

Chapter 1
Starting Points

"Noah endured years of ridicule from those around him as he worked. This righteous man had been spending his family's inheritance and wasting his life for the better part of a century building a massive boat in the middle of nowhere. To make matters worse, it had never even rained on earth, so how could the world ever be flooded? Nevertheless, Noah tirelessly withstood the abuse to faithfully carry out God's plan, and in the end, he and his family survived the Flood while everyone else died."

The above retelling reflects common misconceptions many Christians have about the Flood account. Apart from Noah building the Ark and surviving the Flood with his family, the remaining details are not found in the pages of Scripture. While it is plausible that Noah was mocked by wicked people in his generation, the Bible never includes this detail, and it never states that he worked on it in the middle of nowhere or in a desert. The amount of time it took Noah to complete the Ark was likely much shorter than 100 years, since his sons were probably already grown and married by the time God commanded him to construct the Ark (Genesis 6:14, 18). The idea that it never rained on the earth prior to the Flood is speculative, being based on Genesis 2:5, a verse describing conditions on day 6 prior to the creation of man. Is it a legitimate interpretation of Scripture to apply the unique conditions of the creation week throughout the entire pre-Flood era of over 1,650 years?[1]

Genesis 6:14–16 explains the basic instructions about the Ark that God gave to Noah:

- Make it out of gopherwood
- Make rooms or enclosures in it for the animals
- Cover it inside and out with pitch
- Make it 300 cubits long, 50 cubits wide, and 30 cubits high[2]
- Finish it one cubit from the top (probably a reference to an opening at the top)
- Set a door in the side of the Ark
- Make it with three levels or decks[3]

The Bible provides a few details about the Ark, but there is much we are not told. This fact explains why the embellishments mentioned earlier have been slipped into the biblical account. How did the Ark Encounter approach the topics on which Scripture is silent? Consider the following questions:

- Did Noah's culture possess the technological capabilities to build the Ark?
- How long did it take Noah to build the Ark?
- How many people, if any, assisted with the work?
- Did Noah know how many animals would be on board and how long the Flood would last?
- Did God perform miracles to assist and protect Noah throughout the construction of the Ark and during the Flood?

The Ark Encounter team worked through these questions and so many others to develop plausible solutions. A handful of well-reasoned assumptions guided their decisions.

First, the Bible is the Word of God, so it served as the final authority on matters that it specifically addresses. This means that the truths about the Ark and Flood outlined in Scripture could not be ignored or altered to fit a given model. For example, the Ark's dimensions could not be expanded to accommodate the necessary animals, and they could not be shrunk to reduce the workload of the Ark's occupants.

Second, the Ark Encounter researchers needed to determine just how many details about the Ark the Lord gave Noah. Did He provide thorough plans so that Noah merely needed to prepare the materials and put them together? Did He only give Noah the instructions listed in Scripture, meaning that Noah would need to work out the remaining complex details? The Ark Encounter opted for the latter position — God only gave Noah the instructions mentioned in the Bible. This means Noah was intelligent enough to figure out how to build such a massive boat, or at least hire people with the ability. Such a view should not be surprising since the Bible indicates man was created by God to be intelligent from the beginning. Certainly it is possible that God told Noah more than Scripture reveals, but even if He did, modern readers are not privy to that information.

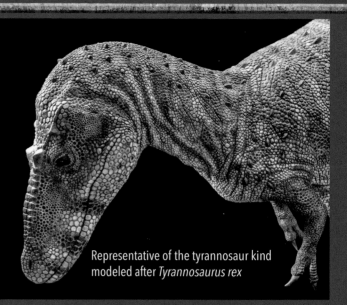

Representative of the tyrannosaur kind modeled after *Tyrannosaurus rex*

Third, since the Bible mentions that only eight people boarded the Ark and survived the Flood, then the Ark must have been seaworthy. The seakeeping of the Ark has been extensively researched by Tim Lovett and other engineers and naval architects. Mr. Lovett has shown that a wooden vessel with the Ark's proportions could indeed survive the worldwide Flood, particularly if it featured certain design elements, such as a bowfin, stern projection, and a multilayered hull. Proving the Ark's seaworthiness is beyond the scope of this work. For more on this subject, please see Tim Lovett's book, *Noah's Ark: Thinking Outside the Box.*

Fourth, the Lord said that the animals would come to Noah to be kept alive on board the Ark (Genesis 6:20). Noah did not have the implausible task of tracking down every kind of animal as often alleged by skeptics in their efforts to mock the biblical account. However, God did tell Noah to bring "all food that is eaten" for his family and the animals (Genesis 6:21). This means that Noah and his family needed to work hard to tend all the animals because God did not miraculously take care of all the details, as some Christians believe.

These two details led to a couple of areas of research for the Ark Encounter team. How many animals were required on the Ark and how could Noah's family provide for all of them? Beginning in 2011, a group of researchers led by Dr. Georgia Purdom of Answers in Genesis has sought to determine the maximum number of animals required to be on the Ark. As chapter 3 will explain, even using "worst-case" assumptions, the total number of animals on board was likely fewer than 7,000.

Using this data, Ark Encounter researchers were able to calculate the space, food, and water requirements for the animals. Since God told Noah to make rooms or nests (Genesis 6:14), the Ark Encounter team set about designing enclosures that would minimize the amount of manual labor involved in the feeding of the animals and their cleanup. Creative solutions and nifty contraptions could have been constructed, but the team remained mindful that the Ark's systems needed to strike a balance between efficiency, reliability, and safety.

Fifth, when thinking about the construction of the Ark and its various systems, one must decide what technological advancements may have been available to Noah. Without evidence of pre-Flood human civilizations in the fossil record, the Ark Encounter team relied on the scant clues found in Scripture. Tubal-Cain was an instructor in bronze and iron, and his half-brother was the leader of those who played the harp and flute (Genesis 4:21–22). We also know that Noah had the know-how to build the Ark. Based on these clues we can see that Noah's culture had achieved a certain level of technological acumen, but just how advanced were they? Ark Encounter researchers determined to picture the technological capabilities of the antediluvian world as being comparable to ancient Greece or Rome. These empires were capable of grand construction projects, including shipbuilding, and like the people of Noah's world, they were extremely corrupt.

The final assumption made by the Ark Encounter researchers is that Noah's Ark has not actually been discovered in recent years. Throughout the construction period, numerous people contacted the Ark Encounter claiming that the real Ark had been found in modern Turkey, so the Ark team should just go look at the original to determine how Noah accomplished his tasks. As amazing as it would be to discover the real Noah's Ark, there has been no solid evidence to verify the claims of its discovery. In fact, the Ark Encounter team believes it is highly unlikely that Noah's Ark still exists since wooden structures do not survive the elements for thousands of years.

Using Scripture as their authority and these six assumptions to guide them, the Ark Encounter team sought to figure out how Noah's family could have accomplished so many important tasks during their year-long stay on the Ark.

Chapter 2
The Ark Through the Ages

"The dimensions of the Ark were ideally designed both for stability and capacity. It has been shown hydrodynamically that the Ark would have been practically impossible to capsize and would have been reasonably comfortable, even during violent waves and winds."

— Dr. Henry Morris,
The Henry Morris Study Bible[1]

When you study the depiction of the Ark in historical images, you will find a vast array of styles — some more practical than others. The Bible gives us only a brief description of dimensions and a couple of other aspects of the Ark's design. This lack of detail has given artists great leeway over the years to stylize the boat and its inhabitants in diverse ways. Many reflect the style of the period the artwork is created in — while others built metaphorical and religious connotations into their designs.

The following examples are shared to reveal how historical figures chose to respond to many of the same questions and objections to the biblical account of Noah's Ark that are still prevalent in the world today. While some of these attempts are clearly off the mark, the Ark Encounter begins with a biblical starting point, and then, with the use of science, research, and historical examples, demonstrates the feasibility of the Ark and its ability to protect Noah's family and representatives of the animal kinds.

St. Augustine ¦354-430 A.D.¦

St. Augustine popularized the allegorical method of interpreting the Bible, but in many cases, he believed the text was both historical and allegorical. In his work, *City of God*, he explained how the animals could fit in the Ark:

"They say, too, that the area of that ark could not contain so many kinds of animals of both sexes, two of the unclean and seven of the clean. But they seem to me to reckon only one area of 300 cubits long and 50 broad, and not to remember that there was another similar in the story above, and yet another as large in the story above that again; and that there was consequently an area of 900 cubits by 150. And if we accept what Origen has with some appropriateness suggested, that Moses the man of God, being, as it is written, 'learned in all the wisdom of the Egyptians,' Acts 7:22 who delighted in geometry, may have meant geometrical cubits, of which they say that one is equal to six of our cubits, then who does not see what a capacity these dimensions give to the ark?"[2]

While Augustine over-calculated by a factor of three, his reminder that the Ark had three levels is on point. Augustine's calculations are wrong. Three levels of 300 x 50 do not equal 900 x 150. Consider, 300 x 50 x 3 = 45,000. 900 x 150 = 135,000. He tripled both figures when he should have only tripled one of them. He went on to discuss the types of animals, their physical needs, housing, and diet:

"Another question is commonly raised regarding the food of the carnivorous animals — whether, without transgressing the command which fixed the number to be preserved, there were necessarily others included in the ark for their sustenance; or, as is more probable, there might be some food which was not flesh, and which yet suited all. For we know how many animals whose food is flesh eat also vegetable products and fruits, especially figs and chestnuts.

What wonder is it, therefore, if that wise and just man was instructed by God what would suit each, so that without flesh he prepared and stored provision fit for every species? And what is there which hunger would not make animals eat? Or what could not be made sweet and wholesome by God, who, with a divine facility, might have enabled them to do without food at all, had it not been requisite to the completeness of so great a mystery that they should be fed?"[3]

Origen ¦c.184-c.253 A.D.¦

Another early Christian writer, Origen, in *Homilies on Genesis and Exodus,* describes the Ark as more pyramidal with a flat top rather than an actual ship, then goes into detail on the internal arrangement of living quarters and storage:

"Now these separations of dwelling places appear to have been made for this reason, that the diverse kinds of animals or beasts could be separated more easily in individual rooms and whatever animals are tame and less active could be divided from the wild beasts. Those separations of dwellings, therefore, are called nests."[4]

As to life on board the Ark, he writes:

". . . since all the animals spent a whole year in the ark, and of course, it was necessary that food be provided that whole year and not only food, but also that places be prepared for wastes so that neither the animals themselves, nor especially the men, be plagued by the stench of excrement. They hand down, therefore, that the lower region itself, which is at the bottom, was given over and set aside for necessities of this kind. But the region above and contiguous to this one was alloted to storing food. And indeed it seemed necessary that animals be brought in from without for those beasts whose nature it was to feed on flesh, that feeding on their flesh they might be able to preserve their life for the sake of renewing offspring, but other provisions would be stored up for other animals, which their natural use demands."[5]

He also wrote *Contra Celsum* as a response to an early critic of Christianity named Celsus who described the history of Noah as ". . . their fantastic story — which they take from the Jews — concerning the flood and the building of an enormous ark, and the business about the message brought back to the survivors of the flood by a dove (or was it an old crow?). This is nothing more than a debased and nonsensical version of the myth of Deucalion, a fact I am sure they would not want to come to light."[6]

The objections to the biblical account have not changed much since Origen's time, and neither has the mockery from skeptics.

Josephus |37-100 A.D.|

Some historians and scholars approached the topic of the Ark as an actual ship designed to be seaworthy and functional. Note the detail and safety recorded in Josephus' account of Noah's Ark:

"… that he should make an ark of four stories high, three hundred cubits long, fifty cubits broad, and thirty cubits high. Accordingly he entered into that ark, and his wife, and sons, and their wives, and put into it not only other provisions, to support

Flavius Josephus

their wants there, but also sent in with the rest all sorts of living creatures, the male and his female, for the preservation of their kinds; and others of them by sevens. Now this ark had firm walls, and a roof, and was braced with cross beams, so that it could not be any way drowned or overborne by the violence of the water. And thus was Noah, with his family, preserved."[7]

Bishop Wilkins |1614-1672 A.D.|

In 1668, Bishop John Wilkins, an Anglican member of the clergy in England, went into great detail to explain the animals and contents of Noah's Ark in his work, *An Essay Towards a Real Character, and a Philosophical Language.* "Bishop John Wilkins took on the 'Atheistical scoffers' who dared say the expanding diversity of the natural world was an argument against 'the truth and authority of Scripture.' … Wilkins' rebuttal … tried to work out exactly how many of which animals would fit in Noah's Ark, a vessel whose dimensions were 'set down to be three hundred cubits in length, fifty in breadth, and thirty in height.' He even made a chart…."[8]

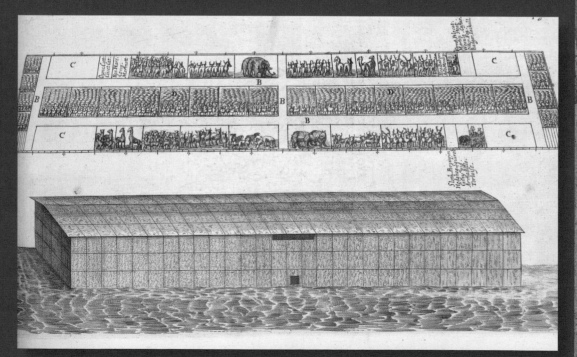

Illustration from Wilkins' essay showing layout and exterior of the Ark; he included charts with numbers of animals categorized by eating hay; fruits, roots, and insects; or being carnivorous. He even went into detail about the capacity of the Ark for animals, their housing, other supplies, and collection of dung.

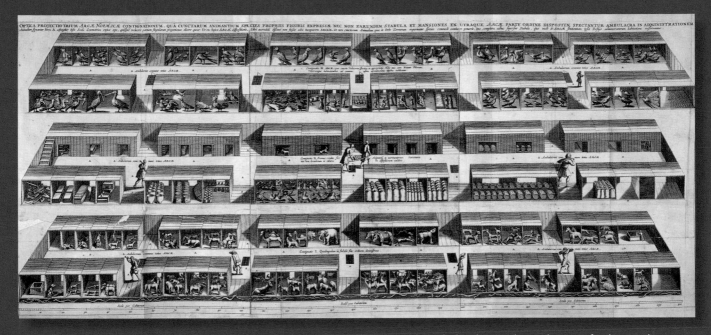

Internal view of Noah's Ark showing the animals housed in their compartments over three decks, along with people caring for them and the storage of supplies.

In 1675, Jesuit German scholar and renowned man of knowledge Anthanasius Kircher collected and shared his research on the biblical account in his book *Arca Noë*. These included his calculations on the vessel's dimensions, as well as addressing popular arguments about overcrowding and questions as to how meat-eating animals on the Ark were fed. Some of his other theories are more fanciful — the inclusion of the creatures called sirens and his thoughts on why snakes were on the Ark as a reminder of the Fall.[9]

"The main focus here is not the Flood, but the vessel. Working its structure out, even to the minutest detail, was a way of making the fundamental laws that govern everything explicit. His reason for giving such a detailed account was not to provide the reader with useful information, but rather to show that everything is consistent. As Kircher explains, Noah was just the fabricator of the Ark; God himself was the architect. Indeed, God went so far as to instill into Noah the knowledge of how to construct the Ark. So the Ark would be a marvelous work, comparable to the seven wonders of the ancient world."[10]

From determining the measurements of a cubit to the mystery of gopherwood, Kircher made detailed analysis and arguments regarding the Ark. His diagrams of the exterior and interior of the ship, down to actual placements of animals and supplies, were equally detailed.

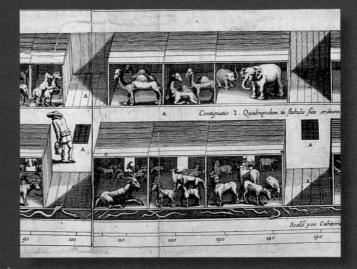

A detail from Kircher's drawing.

Modern Renaissance

Box-like Ark depictions were predominant at the resurgence of the Creationist movement in the early 70s and 80s. As studies about seaworthiness and stability have continued, ship design features have been tested and are now included in many Ark images.

By undertaking the challenge of answering questions about the size, viability, number of animals, layout, and design of the vessel, these historians and theologians defended the truth of the biblical account. While some of their reasoning and calculations may have proven faulty, their attempts remain admirable.

The publication of *The Genesis Flood* by Dr. Henry Morris and Dr. John Whitcomb was a pivotal work in re-introducing the idea of literal truth to the concepts of creation and the global Flood of Genesis. It also discussed Noah's Ark as an actual vehicle by which mankind and representatives of the animal kinds were saved. In Dr. Morris' commentary notes for Genesis 6:16, he states:

> "The three decks may have been laid out as follows: large animals on the bottom; small animals and food storage on the middle deck; family quarters, possessions, records, etc., on the top deck. Water could have been stored in cisterns on the roof and piped throughout the ark where needed. Overhead water storage could also have provided fluid pressure for various other uses."[11]

In 1996, another groundbreaking work related to the Ark was published. In *Noah's Ark: A Feasibility Study,* John Woodmorappe used common-sense solutions to demonstrate how eight people could care for the needs of an estimated 16,000 animals, based on the genus level of taxonomy.

"This work is a systematic evaluation of the housing, feeding, watering, and waste-disposal requirements of some 16,000 animals on Noah's Ark. It is also a comprehensive rebuttal to the myriads of arguments that have been made against the Ark over the centuries. It is shown that it was possible for eight people to care for 16,000 animals, and without miraculous Divine intervention."[12]

Australian researcher Tim Lovett focused attention on the Ark's construction. After years of study and design, Lovett wrote the following:

"The Bible gives the all-important dimensions of the ark, but leaves out many aspects of its construction. This suggested design reflects a stable, comfortable, and seaworthy vessel that was capable of fulfilling all the requirements stated in Genesis. It also makes the most sense of a rather elongated lifeboat."[13]

These books represent a renaissance for creation science, which had fallen out of favor due to the uniformitarian philosophy popularized in the 1800s followed by the prevalence of Charles Darwin's *Origin of Species.* Morris and Whitcomb's work brought into focus the need to bridge the perceived gaps between science and biblical history. Woodmorappe, Lovett, and many others have built upon *The Genesis Flood,* examining relevant subjects in light of new data and diligent study of Scripture. Adding their own research to the mix, the Ark Encounter team produced a life-size Ark that addresses skeptical questions and demonstrates the feasibility of the Flood account.

Could Such a Large Wooden Ship Float?

It is not surprising that few ancient ships can measure up to the noted size of the Ark, even taking into account differing views on the length of a cubit. One of the principal arguments against the viability of the Ark since the early church is its size. However, history has left us intriguing clues about other ships that would come close to rivaling it.

🔹 *Leontifera* — the largest ship of Ceranus engaged in a naval battle in 280 B.C. — powered by 1,600 rowers and estimated between 400 and 500 feet; [The ship] was admired for her "large size and exquisite construction."

🔹 Plutarch's description of Demetrius' fleet — built around 294 B.C., "they had a speed and effectiveness which was more remarkable than their great size" — based on the number of oars per tier, it is estimated to have been over 400 feet in length.

🔹 Athenaeus records several examples of very large ships, including one at 420 feet long and over 70 feet high, built by Ptolemy Philopator and powered by 4,000 rowers [*Tessarakonteres*].[14]

Several views of a replica Antikythera mechanism, an early form of mechanical device.

The Chinese treasure ships of Admiral Zheng He during the Ming Dynasty were also said to have been between 400 and 600 feet in length.

There are also tantalizing clues that ancient Egyptian boats were much more sophisticated and prevalent in their use, because of discoveries of seagoing vessels like those at Mersa/Wadi Gawasis, than assumed from the limited number of other ships recovered at various sites.

Ancient shipwreck sites are also providing additional evidence of the skills of early shipbuilders, including that of the Antikythera wreck,[15] a very large ship that sank over 2,000 years ago.

Wyoming

WOOD SHIPS

| 0 | 100 ft. | 200 ft. | 300 ft. | 400 ft. | 500 ft. |

Noah's Ark

The *Wyoming*, built in 1909, is often discussed in connection with the Ark because its size approaches Noah's vessel. With a deck length of 350 feet (450 feet overall from tip to tip), this schooner was the largest wooden ship in modern times. Skeptics like Bill Nye cite the *Wyoming* in an attempt to dismiss the biblical account as absurd. The *Wyoming* notoriously had several problems due to its size. The long planks of its hull twisted and buckled, which demanded the use of a pump to bail water from the hold. Tragically, the *Wyoming* sank in 1924, and all 14 people on board were lost at sea.

Several details are often ignored by skeptics when discussing the *Wyoming*. First, the *Wyoming* and many other large wooden ships built around the same time were "commercial workhorses built as quickly as possible and with an expected working life of only 12–15 years or as little as ten."[16] Second, as mentioned earlier, several ancient wooden ships were reportedly close to the size of the Ark. These were apparently constructed with stronger hulls that allowed them to overcome the problems faced by the *Wyoming*. Finally, the *Wyoming* carried thousands of tons of coal along the Atlantic coast for nearly 15 years! The Ark needed to float for a maximum of five months before landing on a mountain in the region of Ararat (Genesis 8:4).

Chapter 3
Could It Work?

"The worst waves may have been caused by wind, just like today. After several months at sea, God made a wind to pass over the earth. This suggests a large-scale weather pattern likely to produce waves with a dominant direction. . . . Once the Ark points into the waves, the long proportions create a more comfortable and controlled voyage. It had no need for speed, but the Ark did 'move about on the surface of the waters.'"

— Tim Lovett[1]

The Flood is an event that is unprecedented in Earth's history. The Ark had a very unique mission compared to other ancient vessels. It is clear that the Ark Encounter does not shy away from the truth — at 510 feet in length, 85 feet in width, and 51 feet in height, the all-wood, life-size Ark is simply immense. It would take roughly 450 semi-trailers to equal its storage capacity of nearly two million cubic feet![2]

Experts at the Ark Encounter, thanks to a multi-year study[3] of animal kinds, including those that have become extinct, have determined the "total number of living and extinct kinds of land animals and flying creatures to be about 1,400. With a 'worst-case' scenario approach to calculating the number of animals on the Ark, this would mean that Noah cared for fewer than 7,000 animals."[4] This would include around 80 of the dinosaur kinds.

Yet the Ark Encounter goes far beyond just the math to present simple, ancient solutions for caring for the animals and Noah's family on board during the journey. It presents an opportunity to share scientific information that proves the Ark could have functioned and survived the journey, just as we learn in God's Word. We will explore these solutions in depth in the following chapters.

How Many Animals Were in the Ark?

A representative of the spinosaur kind modeled after *Baryonyx*.

"Of the birds after their kind, of animals after their kind, and of every creeping thing of the earth after its kind, two of every kind will come to you to keep them alive." —Genesis 6:20

One of the most important issues relating to the Flood is the topic of animals on the Ark. The estimated numbers, sizes, and types of Ark animals impacts nearly every aspect of the vessel's interior operations, including time and labor expenditures, food and water needs, space and waste management, and enclosure design. The subject of fitting all the required animals on the Ark is a significant point of contention between biblical creationists and skeptics.

However, providing that information is a bit more complicated than compiling data about different animal species. First we have to answer some fundamental questions.

Which Animals Were Brought into the Ark?
The Bible informs us that Noah brought representatives of every land-dependent, air-breathing animal — ones that could not otherwise survive the Flood (Genesis 7:21–23). Conversely, Noah did not preserve marine animals — or likely even insects — since most of them could survive outside the Ark. Also, insects take in oxygen through spiracles in their skin rather than breathing through nostrils.

How Many Species Are in the World Today?
Skeptics often assert that there are millions of species in the world — far more than could fit on the Ark. However, according to estimates published in 2014, there are fewer than 1.8 million documented species of organisms in the world. Consider also that over 98 percent of those species are fish, invertebrates, and non-animals (like plants and bacteria). This means that there are fewer than 34,000 species of known, land-dependent vertebrates in the world today.

Species or Kinds?
Though wild animals today are often considered according to their *species,* the Bible deals with animals according to their *min* — a common Hebrew word usually translated "kind." We can infer from Scripture that God created plants and animals to reproduce after their kinds (Genesis 1:11–25), and it is clear from various texts that a kind is often a broader category than the current concept of a species. This means that a kind may contain many different species. Since Noah was only sent select representatives from relevant kinds, all land-dwelling vertebrate species not present on the Ark were wiped out. Therefore, if we see an Ark kind represented today by different species — e.g. horses, zebras, and donkeys of the equid kind — those species have developed since the time of the Flood. Therefore, species are simply varying expressions of a particular kind.

Representative of the caseid kind modeled after *Cotylorhyncus.*

What Is an Animal Kind?

There are numerous approaches to defining a kind, but one of the simplest is 'a creationally distinct type of organism and all its descendants.'

Kinds are often referred to as baramins (from the Hebrew words for "created" and "kind"), and the study of created kinds is called baraminology.

What Are the Criteria for Identifying Kinds?

In 2011, Ark Encounter researchers began in-depth animal studies with the goal of identifying the maximum number of Ark kinds. The researchers applied three primary criteria in estimating the Ark kinds: hybridization, cognitum, and statistical baraminology.

Hybrid data is the most-favored method in identifying kinds. Researchers believe that only closely related animals can successfully produce offspring, and this is consistent with the Bible's emphasis on the relationship between reproduction and created kinds. Since only animals in the same kind are related, hybrids positively identify which animals are part of the same kind. The usefulness of hybrid data is limited, however, in that not all potential crosses have been tested or reliably documented. Hybridization is also strictly an *inclusive criterion,* as not even all related animals can produce offspring together.

The cognitum approach estimates animal kinds using the human senses of perception. This method assumes that animal kinds have maintained their core distinctiveness even as they have diversified over time. Presently, extinct animals are most often classified using this approach. For example, wooly mammoths are extinct and there are no hybrid data connecting them with elephants. However, their extreme similarity to elephants has resulted in their placement in the elephant kind.

In statistical analyses, continuities and discontinuities of animals are identified by comparing physical traits using statistical tests called baraminic distance correlation (BDC). Like the cognitum approach, this method assumes that the physical similarities and dissimilarities identified in the tests are reliable indictors of relatedness. It also assumes that the traits selected for comparison are baraminologically significant.

What Are Some Safeguards Against Underestimating the Ark Animals?

The Ark Encounter researchers put several safeguards in place to avoid underestimating the number of animals on the Ark. These include a tendency to split rather than lump animal groups. Also, all "clean" and all flying creatures — not just "clean" ones — were multiplied by fourteen instead of seven animals.

What Are "Splitting" and "Lumping"?

Estimating the number of animals on the Ark depends upon several factors. Near the top of that list is the decision to "split" or "lump" the animals that may or may not be related as a kind.

Coyotes, wolves, dingoes, and domestic dogs can generally interbreed. Thus, they can be "lumped" into the same kind. So, Noah just needed two members of the dog kind on the Ark.

Representatives of the pig kind modeled after *Platygonus.*

18

On the other hand, there are approximately two dozen known families of bats, living and extinct. Based on anatomy and other features, many of these families probably belong to the same kind. In fact, it is possible that every bat belongs to the same kind. However, since breeding studies have not yet confirmed this idea, the data here has "split" the bats into their various families. So, instead of including as few as 14 bats on the Ark, the information depicts over 300 of them (14 from each family).

In keeping with the worst-case approach to estimating the number of animals on the Ark, the animals will be "split" into separate kinds whenever the data is insufficient to support "lumping" them into a single kind.

Why Fourteen Instead of Seven Animals?

Some Bible translations indicate that Noah was to bring seven of each flying creature and clean animal. Yet other Bibles state that seven pairs of these creatures were on the Ark.

Seven of each kind:	Seven pairs of each kind:
KJV*	NLT
NKJV	ESV*
NASB*	HCSB
NET*	NRSV
NIV (1984)*	NIV (2011)

* Asterisks indicate that a textual note appears in these Bibles that mentions the possibility of the other view.

The Hebrew text literally reads, "seven seven — a male and his female" (Genesis 7:2). Does this unique phrasing mean seven or fourteen?

In favor of the "seven" view is that Genesis 8:20 states that Noah sacrificed clean animals and birds after the Flood. While it doesn't say that Noah sacrificed just one animal of each clean kind, those who hold to the "seven" view could point to the common "six and one" pattern seen in the Old Testament. For example, God created the world in six days and rested for one (Genesis 1; Exodus 20:11). Perhaps six of each clean animal were for man's use and one was dedicated to the Lord.

In favor of the "seven pairs" view is the text's mention that there would be a male and "his female" for the clean animals. If an odd number was brought to Noah, then

Representative of the bear kind modeled after *Agriotherium*.

plenty of animals did not have a mate. Furthermore, the Hebrew text does not use similar wording with the unclean animals in verse two. That is, readers can know that one pair of unclean animals was in view, but the text does not say "two two, a male and his female" — it just has the word for two.

Since Hebrew language scholars do not agree about this issue, it seems wise to be tentative about which view is accurate. Since a worst-case approach is being used in regard to the animals, these calculations are based on the "seven pairs" position.

What Is Meant by a "Worst-Case Scenario?"

The Ark Encounter depicts a worst-case approach when estimating the number of animal kinds. Some people believe Noah brought two of every unclean animal and seven of every clean animal.

The text seems to indicate that Noah cared for more animals than this, particularly when it comes to the clean animals and flying creatures. The Lord may have sent seven pairs of the clean animals and seven pairs of all the flying creatures (not just the clean varieties; Genesis 7:2-3).

Although this worst-case approach more than doubles the estimated number of animals on the Ark, this model shows that even a high-end estimate of total animals would have fit on board. Obviously, if the Lord sent just seven of each clean animal and seven of just the clean flying creatures, the Ark would have had plenty of space to accommodate this lower total.

How Many Animal Kinds Were on the Ark?

Based on initial projections, the Ark Encounter team estimates that there were fewer than 1,400 animal kinds on the Ark. It is anticipated that future research may reduce that number even further.

How Many Individual Animals Were on the Ark?

The Ark Encounter team projects that there were fewer than 7,000 animals on board the Ark. The wide discrepancy between the number of Ark kinds and Ark individuals is due to the relatively large number of flying and "clean" kinds — each estimated at 14 animals apiece rather than two.

Living	Kinds (est.)	Per Kind	Total (est.)
Amphibians	194	2	388
Reptiles	101	2	202
Mammals	136	2, 14 ("clean" or powered flight)	644
Birds	195	2, 14 (powered flight)	2,670

Extinct	Kinds (est.)	Per Kind	Total (est.)
"Amphibians"	54	2	108
"Reptiles"	219	2, 14 (powered flight)	726
Synapsids (non-mammalian)	78	2	156
Mammals	332	2, 14 ("clean" or powered flight)	844
Birds	90	2, 14 (powered flight)	1,020
*Total	1,399		6,758

*Figures vary slightly from first edition to accomodate latest research

How Big Were the Ark Animals?

Even when massive dinosaurs and giant elephant-like creatures are factored in, the Ark animals were probably much smaller than is frequently assumed. According to estimates provided by the Ark Encounter, it is projected only 15 percent of Ark animals achieved an adult mass over 22 pounds (10 kg). This means that the vast majority of Ark animals were smaller than a beagle, with most of those being much smaller. Starting with a mass category of 0.035–0.35 oz. (1–10 g), the animal groups were broken up into eight logarithmically increasing size classes. Amazingly, the size range with the greatest projected number of Ark animals was 0.35–3.5 oz. (10–100 g).

Representative of the azhdarchid kind modeled after *Quetzalcoatlus*

Representatives of the rhinoceros kind, modeled after *Trigonias*

Were the Animals Caged?

Some people assume that the Ark animals were free to roam the Ark, but there are problems with this idea. First, it would not be safe for the animals on a vessel that surely rocked and pitched in the stormy seas. Second, as mentioned earlier, there is no guarantee that all of the Ark's animals were vegetarian. Finally, and most importantly, the Lord told Noah to "make rooms in the ark" (Genesis 6:14). Some Bibles use "nests" instead of "rooms." Essentially, Noah was to make enclosures for the Ark's animals.

A cage or pen system was the easiest way to ensure every animal remained safe and received care. How many pens would have been needed? Part of the answer is determined by the number of kinds on board and how they may have been placed as part of the vessel. The Ark Encounter team notes: "If the animals were placed into enclosures by kind (two per enclosure or 14 per enclosure depending on the kind), and using the current projection of 1,399 kinds, then we're looking at 1,399 enclosures."[5]

Representatives of the hyena kind modeled after *Ictitherium*.

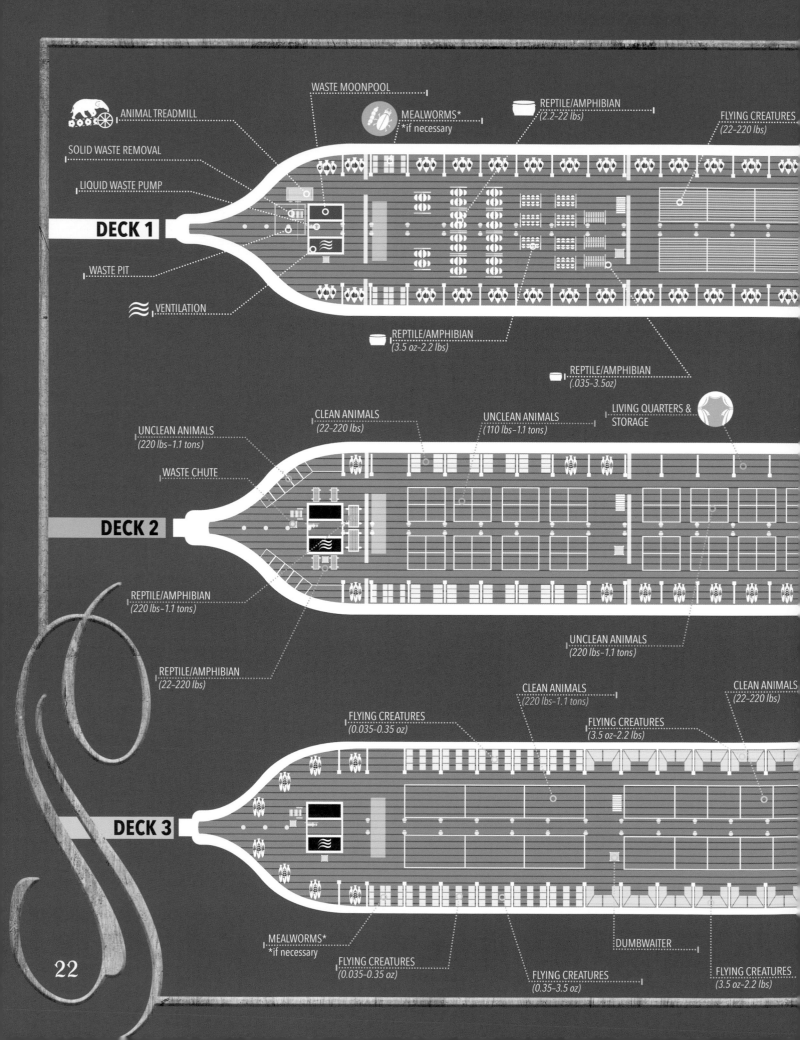

ANIMAL TREADMILL

SOLID WASTE REMOVAL

LIQUID WASTE PUMP

DECK 1

WASTE PIT

≈ VENTILATION

WASTE MOONPOOL

MEALWORMS*
*if necessary

REPTILE/AMPHIBIAN
(2.2–22 lbs)

FLYING CREATURES
(22–220 lbs)

REPTILE/AMPHIBIAN
(3.5 oz–2.2 lbs)

REPTILE/AMPHIBIAN
(.035–3.5oz)

UNCLEAN ANIMALS
(220 lbs–1.1 tons)

WASTE CHUTE

CLEAN ANIMALS
(22–220 lbs)

UNCLEAN ANIMALS
(110 lbs–1.1 tons)

LIVING QUARTERS &
STORAGE

DECK 2

REPTILE/AMPHIBIAN
(220 lbs–1.1 tons)

REPTILE/AMPHIBIAN
(22–220 lbs)

UNCLEAN ANIMALS
(220 lbs–1.1 tons)

CLEAN ANIMALS
(220 lbs–1.1 tons)

CLEAN ANIMALS
(22–220 lbs)

FLYING CREATURES
(0.035–0.35 oz)

FLYING CREATURES
(3.5 oz–2.2 lbs)

DECK 3

MEALWORMS*
*if necessary

FLYING CREATURES
(0.035–0.35 oz)

FLYING CREATURES
(0.35–3.5 oz)

DUMBWAITER

FLYING CREATURES
(3.5 oz–2.2 lbs)

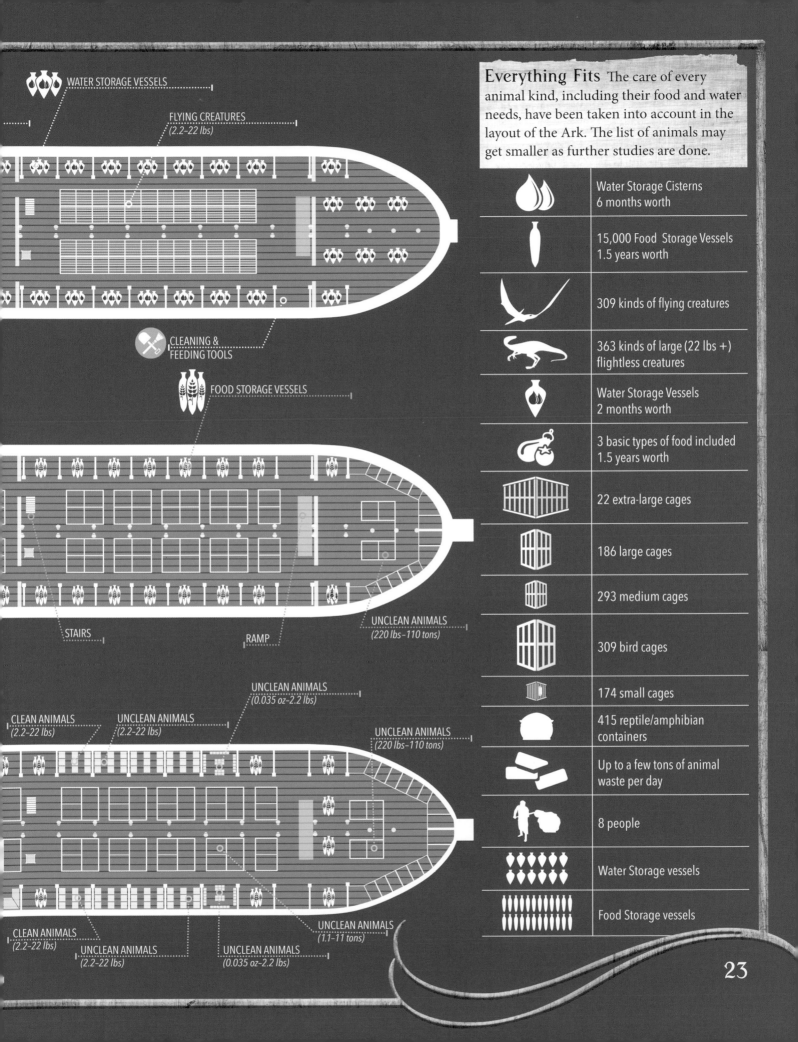

WATER STORAGE VESSELS

FLYING CREATURES
(2.2–22 lbs)

CLEANING &
FEEDING TOOLS

FOOD STORAGE VESSELS

STAIRS

RAMP

UNCLEAN ANIMALS
(220 lbs–110 tons)

UNCLEAN ANIMALS
(0.035 oz–2.2 lbs)

CLEAN ANIMALS
(2.2–22 lbs)

UNCLEAN ANIMALS
(2.2–22 lbs)

UNCLEAN ANIMALS
(220 lbs–110 tons)

CLEAN ANIMALS
(2.2–22 lbs)

UNCLEAN ANIMALS
(2.2–22 lbs)

UNCLEAN ANIMALS
(0.035 oz–2.2 lbs)

UNCLEAN ANIMALS
(1.1–11 tons)

Everything Fits The care of every animal kind, including their food and water needs, have been taken into account in the layout of the Ark. The list of animals may get smaller as further studies are done.

Water Storage Cisterns 6 months worth
15,000 Food Storage Vessels 1.5 years worth
309 kinds of flying creatures
363 kinds of large (22 lbs +) flightless creatures
Water Storage Vessels 2 months worth
3 basic types of food included 1.5 years worth
22 extra-large cages
186 large cages
293 medium cages
309 bird cages
174 small cages
415 reptile/amphibian containers
Up to a few tons of animal waste per day
8 people
Water Storage vessels
Food Storage vessels

Chapter 4
Food & Water Storage

"And you shall take for yourself of all food that is eaten, and you shall gather it to yourself; and it shall be food for you and for them."

— Genesis 6:21

The Lord instructed Noah to bring enough food to feed his family and all the animals during their time on the Ark. Once the number of animals is known, three significant problems need to be solved. How much food would need to be gathered? What types of food would need to be gathered? How could they store so much food?

At the Ark Encounter, you will see a small garden area near the kitchen of the Ark. This garden includes a variety of plants that may have been able to grow in low-light conditions and might have been used to supplement the diets of the people and animals on board.

"Long before the Flood began, Noah may have begun preserving seeds and cultivating plants so that there would be fresh food to eat during the one year voyage. Noah may have potted seedlings to preserve the useful trees and shrubs too. The Ark's upper deck beneath the long window may have been specially designed to accommodate these plants, turning part of the Ark into a vast greenhouse.

Most plants could have survived outside the Ark upon floating rafts of vegetation as seeds and as debris that could have been propagated as cuttings in the mud left behind by the retreating waters."[1]

How Much Food?

The question regarding the amount of food depends on several key factors. First, how many animals would be on board? As shown in the previous chapter, using worst-case assumptions, the Ark Encounter team estimates that fewer than 7,000 individual creatures would have boarded the Ark.

The amount of food required also depends on how much the animals need to survive. Using the average mass of the various categories and types of animals allowed the Ark Encounter researchers to estimate the amount of food and water that each creature would consume per day. The Ark team did not assume that God miraculously put all the animals into hibernation, as supposed by some creationists.

One more piece of information is required to determine the amount of food Noah needed to store. How long would they be on the Ark? As mentioned in the Introduction, the Ark Encounter adopted the position that the only information the Lord gave to Noah was recorded in Scripture. Since Scripture does not record God telling Noah how long the Flood would last, then the Ark team assumed that Noah did not know this information.

If Noah did not know how long the Flood would last, how could he possibly know how much food to store? It is quite possible that he did not know how much food

to bring on the Ark, but someone certainly knew. God knows everything. He knew exactly how long Noah's family and the animals would be on the Ark, and He knew how large the Ark would need to be to house all of the people, animals, and supplies for the allotted time. So, even if Noah was not sure how long they would be on the Ark, he trusted that God's instructions would be sufficient.

Assuming the above reasoning, it seems that Noah would have simply loaded the Ark with as much food as possible, allowing space for other necessities, such as the animal enclosures, working spaces, and living quarters. While constructing the "Half Ark Model" for an exhibit in the Ark Encounter, researchers discovered that everything fit nicely (see pages 22-23 "Everything Fits"), even allowing for a small excess of food.

This finding should not surprise Bible-believing Christians. While some creationists have assumed the Ark had plenty of leftover space, often said to be for the people who refused Noah's alleged invitation, the Ark Encounter team found that this just isn't the case. The Ark was just the right size to house the animals and their required food for one year. Think about it. Does it make any sense to think that God instructed Noah to spend years of his life building an Ark that was far larger than necessary?

What Types of Food?

And God said, "See, I have given you every herb that yields seed which is on the face of all the earth, and every tree whose fruit yields seed; to you it shall be for food. Also, to every beast of the earth, to every bird of the air, and to everything that creeps on the earth, in which there is life, I have given every green herb for food"; and it was so (Genesis 1:29–30).

After making everything, the Lord stated that people and animals were to eat vegetation. It was not until after the Flood that God permitted man to eat meat (Genesis 9:3). We cannot be sure when certain animals began to eat meat, although the fossil record provides strong evidence that carnivory occurred prior to the Flood.

If carnivorous activity was prevalent in the pre-Flood world, it is still possible that the animals the Lord sent did not eat meat or that they could have survived for one year without meat. There have been modern examples of animals normally considered to be carnivores that refused to eat meat, such as the lion named Little Tyke.[2]

However, if some of the Ark's animals did eat meat, there are several methods of preserving or supplying their food. Meat can be preserved through drying, smoking, salting, or pickling. Certain fish can pack themselves in mud and survive for years without water — these could have been stored on the Ark. Mealworms and other insects can be bred for both carnivores and insectivores.

Many, if not all, of the animals were vegetarian. To provide food for all of these animals, Noah's family could have grown or purchased vast stores of grains, grasses, seeds, and nuts. Certain vegetables with a long shelf life may have been brought aboard, as could dried varieties of some fruits and vegetables.

What about Picky Eaters?

When you look at the animals in the world today, many of them cannot simply be classified as either an herbivore (plant eater) or carnivore (meat eater). Also, some animals today have special needs that require specific handling. How could Noah's family provide for these types of animals? Remember that today's animals are descendants of the Ark representatives and many modern animals are likely more specialized in their dietary and habitat needs.

Koala

Take the modern koala for example. Koalas can eat the leaves of some other trees, such as the wattle, paperbark, and tea trees, but they prefer certain eucalyptus leaves. Like other animals, the koala's Ark ancestors were less specialized, like *Litokoala*, and probably heartier than modern representatives. As such, they may have eaten a much wider variety of food, including grains, fruits, and vegetables.

As their name suggests, anteaters thrive on eating ants and can devour up to 35,000 insects a day. However, anteaters in captivity are often fed fruit and eggs. In the wild, giant anteaters also consume fruit that has dropped to the ground, while other anteater species can climb trees to get fruit.

So when looking at the animal kinds we know today, it is important to keep in mind that the variations of the original animal kinds in our world today may be more specialized or adapted to specific environments than the Ark's animals were at the time. We cannot assume these limitations for the animal kinds on the Ark.

What about Creatures with Specialized Needs?

This also extends to animals with specialized needs, like those seen in hippos today. They have skin that needs to be kept wet most of the time, and they secrete a reddish substance that helps to keep them from getting sunburned. Of course, being kept inside the Ark would protect them from sunburn, but their skin can still dry out. The Ark had plenty of water, so it's possible that Noah's family developed a system to regularly deliver water to keep the hippos moist. These creatures may not have been as difficult to tend as many people imagine.

There are two species of the hippo kind in the world today. The animal most people think of is the common hippopotamus, but there is also the pygmy hippo. The pygmy hippo is more terrestrial, though still semi-aquatic, and they appear to be much more like the fossil hippos found in early post-Flood rock layers. So, the Ark's hippos were likely smaller and more terrestrial than the large common hippos.

How Could the Food Be Stored?

Strategic placement of food would also minimize the effort needed to retrieve and distribute it.

Food and water takes up most of the bays, but several rooms on each of the three decks could have been used for additional small cages, mealworm cultivation, and miscellaneous storage. Placing the food in large silos, bags, or other corruptible containers would increase the possibility of spoilage and waste. Using sealed earthen vessels would protect against moisture, mold, or rotting.

The designs of the water and food storage vessels are based on a re-occurring design that we see throughout history. This design shows up in various cultures from Greece to China at different times because it works

well for shipping goods, and because the vessels are made from a material that is readily available — clay. There could have been other storage methods such as barrels, bags, crates, etc., but when weighing simplicity of production, short-term needs, and the need to keep goods free of contaminants, earthenware makes a lot of sense.

Based on the projected number of animals and their calculated food needs at 80 percent dry matter along with a 50 percent contingency (oversupply in case of spoilage or miscalculations), the hypothetical layout contains nearly 15,000 earthen vessels, each with a volume of 1.75 cubic feet (50 cm³).

Earthenware storage roped together for stability

In the history of ships and ocean voyages, water collection has been documented using runoff from the sails or through use of barrels on deck. Neither technique is one that would work on the Ark, so what would? The Ark could have served as a huge rainwater collection device with a simple system, such as:
❶ rainwater falling on the roof and deck surface is ❷ channeled into ❸ cisterns where it is stored and distributed as needed, such as to the ❹ watering vessels in the animal pens and cages.

How Could the Water Be Stored?

With a strong, seaworthy vessel full of the necessary supplies, the next most important aspect of the adventure would be the availability of fresh water for drinking and removal of waste products during the journey. Water has always been at the heart of any civilization. On the Ark it would have been needed for drinking for both the people and the animals. Water would also have been required for bathing and for washing clothes and dishes. Noah's family could have used it to clean out some of the animal stalls, and some of the amphibians would have occasionally needed their water to be switched out.

For this journey, Noah faced a number of challenges related to water management. How many animals would be cared for? How much water would be needed? How would they maintain sanitary conditions on board? Would the Ark be able to carry enough water for the duration of the Flood? We have already looked at the number of animals and how much food may have been required. Based on the number of animals, their sizes, and their activity level, we can also calculate the amount of water they would have needed.

Possible Solutions?

Unlike ancient sailors who often relied on staying close to shore or planned stops at islands during long ocean voyages, Noah faced a world that would be completely covered by an ocean. There are numerous examples of early civilizations boiling water or using sand as a filter to acquire safe water. Developing a large-scale method of filtration for the Ark would have been a monumental feat. Assuming Noah did not develop such a process and that the Lord did not miraculously filter the water for them, the Ark Encounter team thought up some other solutions to ensure the Ark had enough fresh water.

Two potential solutions were considered:

1   Carry: The Ark carried all of the required water on board to meet the needs of the animals and people during the time on board, which was approximately one year.

2   Collect: The Ark carried or stored large quantities of water in cisterns on board but required secondary means to regularly replenish these tanks.

As we explore each premise, it will become clear why the Ark Encounter chose the second option.

Carry

In his feasibility study of the Ark, John Woodmorappe calculated the amount of water for approximately 16,000 animals (based on the genus level). In his computations, he assumed all water had to be carried on board and concluded that 4.07 million liters of water (over 1 million gallons) would be needed. The storage of this amount of water would take up slightly less than 10 percent of the volume of the Ark.[3] A variety of storage methods could have been used, such as cisterns, water storage containers, or vessels.

With the Ark Encounter's more in-depth study on the number of animal kinds aboard the Ark, the amount of water needed might have been even less. However, even if Woodmorappe's calculations are fairly accurate, the Ark Encounter team identified two problems with this approach. First, it would be extremely difficult to prevent the contamination of so much standing water over the course of a year. If Noah relied upon stored water for the entire trip, the contamination of the water source would be catastrophic.

Second, this method goes against one of the basic assumptions made by the Ark Encounter team described in the introduction. They assumed that God did not tell Noah how long they would be on the Ark. Noah would need to know this detail if he planned to construct and fill all of the containers required to hold the necessary water. One might assume that he could have simply trusted that God knew how large the Ark would need to be in order to hold the storage tanks and vessels (as mentioned regarding food storage), but this unknown creates another variable that could have been eliminated by utilizing a different system for obtaining water.

Collect

When viewing the floorplans for the Half-Ark Model (chapter 3), you can see that cisterns are included on the second and third decks along each side of the ship, not far from the animal pens and enclosures. There are also many sealed earthen vessels on the first deck that hold a two-month supply of potable water. The cistern design is meant to utilize rainfall during the Flood to provide the required amounts of water.

This series of cisterns with a reliable dispersion system could have stored all of the water necessary for the Ark's occupants without additional water storage as cargo.[4] The earthenware images for the Ark Encounter are not representative of mass water storage. These would likely have stored food or other items, or were utilized in post-cistern distribution or containment of smaller amounts of water for specific use.

One inch of water collected on the Ark's roof would have filled nearly one week's worth of water needs (assuming the roof could collect every drop that landed on it).[5] If the various cisterns were sized and distributed per the needs of the animals[6] housed in specific areas of the Ark, this would have helped with overall water distribution and collection.

The Ark had more than enough space to comfortably house cisterns large enough for a six-month supply. Would there have been enough rain to sustain these cisterns? Experts at the Ark Encounter note the amount needed is the same as the average precipitation in Kentucky and that "the evaporation of warm floodwaters would have likely caused more than enough rain to fall during the remainder of Noah's time on the Ark, ensuring they had plenty of water."[7] To prevent overflowing the cisterns due to excess rain, a series of valves and spigots could have been used to shut off the flow of water from the Ark's roof.

Cutaway view of water distribution on the Ark, showing ❶ cisterns, ❷ spigots with handle that could be turned to control the flow of the water, ❸ bamboo piping within the Ark's structure, and ❹ watering vessels for the animal kinds.

Chapter 5
Feeding & Watering

"Exploring natural solutions for day-to-day operations does not discount God's role: the biblical account hints at plenty of miracles as written, such as God bringing the animals to the Ark. . . . It turns out that a study of existing, low-tech animal care methods answers trivial objections to the Ark."[1]

— John Woodmorappe

Having explored the water and food needs for the journey, the next questions inevitably center around how the animals on board were cared for during the journey. What you see at the Ark Encounter really comes down to two important concepts – workable models for solutions and how these helped make the workload manageable for the limited human labor available.

Providing care for such a diverse groups of creatures would have involved a lot of work for the family of eight, but there are simple, time-tested solutions that work to reduce the chores. Based on the calculations of the Ark Encounter team, each family member would have been responsible for around 850 animals. This would have included feeding, watering, and caring for any injuries the animals may have incurred.

Pipes and Joints

Distributing water for the Ark's needs, such as small animals, larger animals, and human living spaces, will vary. It would have been highly inefficient and unnecessarily toilsome for the family members to carry large containers of water around all day. Utilizing a system of bamboo piping and spigots would allow the water to reach the animal pens, gardens, and living quarters.

While other technologies may have been available, the Ark Encounter chose to use bamboo piping because it occurs naturally and is still used today in geographic areas where metal or ceramic pipes are impractical.[2] Plus, bamboo is lightweight, so replacement piping could easily be stored without adding much mass to the overall Ark load.

Bamboo pipes can be easily fitted together using several types of joints and lashings. These can include simple holes drilled in the bamboo and then lashings like leather strips, rope, or waterproofed material that is fastened and secured to keep the piping in place together. It is best to use bamboo that is dry, and while simple to complete, the bamboo will split or become damaged if you don't use care in positioning and forming the joints properly.

Representative of the macraucheniid kind modeled after *Theosodon*

Cages for the large animals (shown above), with the exception of large birds, have flat floors. Transfer systems could be easily incorporated into the design, so it would have been safe for Noah's family to clean them. See Chapter 6 for additional details on the simple transfer system designed by the Ark Encounter team. The animals shown here are representatives of the rebbachisaur kind modeled after *Nigersaurus*.

Large-Animal Enclosures

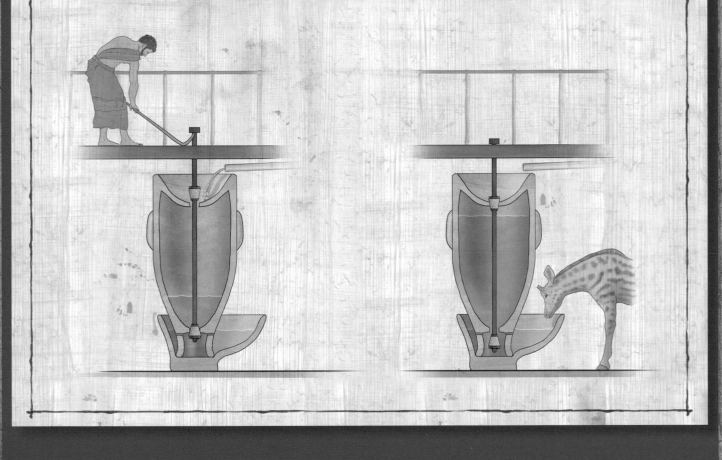

Water collected from the roof may have been stored in cisterns and then transferred through bamboo piping to smaller tanks. Valves and spigots could be used to control water flow into and out of these large clay vessels near the animal enclosures.

The large-animal water distribution is more involved than the system for the smaller animals. The Ark Encounter developed a system that allows one person to go through and water the large animal cages through a series of pipes and spigots that fill up large vacuum-fed water tanks.

All this could be accomplished through a catwalk running above the animal enclosures. This design accomplishes significant time and labor savings, as these larger animals — 22 lbs. (10 kg) or greater — represent around 15 percent of the Ark's population and occupy an even larger percentage of the ship's floor space. Working in two-person teams is probably the most efficient arrangement, but an advantage of utilizing partially automated systems is that single tasks do not always require the attention of both individuals. This is critical since the Ark only contained eight laborers.

Water could be turned on and off via simple spigots to fill up large water tanks within each group of large animal cages. These earthen tanks operate on the same basic principles as modern water dispensers for chickens. The water is primarily held by vacuum in a vertical tank, which then replenishes a lower bowl as the animal drinks. Rather than rotating the vessel upside-down for refilling, a design featuring a central rod with double-corks could allow for a safe and efficient accomplishment of the task. Prying the rod upward breaks the vacuum seal from the top, while a cork at the bottom simultaneously seals the outlet. Once the water is topped-off, the rod could be hammered back down, reversing the seal and restoring the vacuum.

Small Animal Enclosures

According to data produced by the Ark Encounter team, 85 percent of the Ark's animals were smaller than a beagle. Thus, the small animal water containers were numerous and efficiency was crucial.

For these cages, the family could have filled water vessels from the main cisterns and taken them by way of cart to the various small cages throughout the Ark.

Each of the water feeders are designed as vacuum-fed vessels. As the animal drinks from the water bowl, the tank above replaces the water bowl. This cuts down on the frequent refilling of the container, thus saving precious time.

The reptile and amphibian enclosures would not typically need frequent refilling since their activity and nutritional needs would have been minimal. It may have been necessary to occasionally use a little bit of water to wash out their enclosures.

A grouping of the small animal enclosures; below are details of the design features

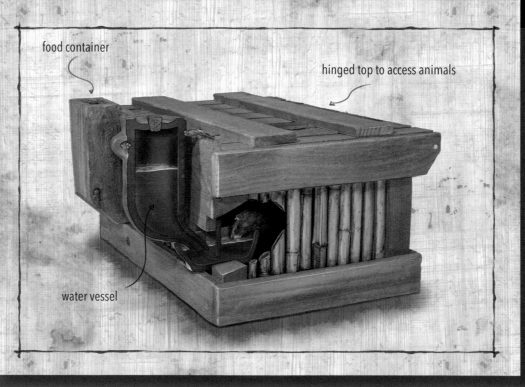

food container

hinged top to access animals

water vessel

36

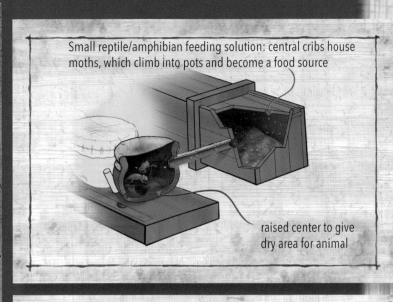

Small reptile/amphibian feeding solution: central cribs house moths, which climb into pots and become a food source

raised center to give dry area for animal

clean water poured through fabric coverings

corks removed to empty liquid waste

waste collected in drainage system

Feeding Systems

The feeding systems on the Ark would have been much easier to develop than the water systems. For large animals, simple funneled chutes leading to the food dish can be filled from the catwalk level.[3] The chutes could be wood or bamboo and use a woven funnel secured to the top. Empty food containers could be repurposed, stored, or eventually discarded. The small animal cages have a small feeding chute that could quickly be filled when necessary.

Large feeders could hold several days' worth of pelletized food and dried vegetation. These foods could be stored on the mezzanine near the large animal cages, allowing someone to quickly refill the feeders from above. Filling tall food chutes from above supplies animals with food for many days.

Chapter 6
Wastewater Systems

"There was careful preparation, and not hurried, thoughtless activity. He prepared the right materials; he prepared the different parts so as to fit together: he prepared his mind, and then prepared his work."

— Charles H. Spurgeon[1]

I t is a simple but unpleasant fact of life — both humans and animals produce liquid and solid waste. Without an effective management system for removal of this waste from living areas, people and animals can sicken and die. Put a large number of animals with eight people in a closed environment like the Ark for about a year during the Flood, and it is a huge challenge that had to be addressed before the journey began.

It is inevitable that there would have been a solution on board the ship for a number of reasons. (1) The design of the vessel was not meant for either crew or animals to be walking about on the roof of the Ark, at least not while it was afloat. The only decks that could be walked on safely on a regular basis during the Flood event were interior ones. (2) While there is a door noted for the Ark, it likely could not be opened during transit.[2] (3) There was an opening at the top of the Ark, but nothing hints at this being a site that waste products could be efficiently tossed out of without landing on areas of the roof and causing sanitation problems. More importantly, if Noah's family collected rainwater from the roof for their water supply, as discussed previously, they would not want to pollute it with sewage. (4) The amount of labor it would take to remove the waste using various types of manual labor alone would have been difficult but manageable. The system solutions for human waste and animal waste could have been completely different, but they may have had a common collection point and labor-reducing method of removal from the ship.

Human Waste — Toilets on the Ark

Flush toilets are not a modern invention nor are large wastewater systems that were used in large ancient cities. These are found at numerous sites of some of the earliest civilizations that have been discovered, including Crete, China, and the Indus Valley. The technology is a very simple one — a seat with an opening that waste falls through, a dispersal method to a collection point,[3] then removal. Sometimes, these were constructed to allow continuous water flow from nearby rivers or other sources to flush the system.

On the Ark itself, dispersal could have taken place by a variety of means using water, from either a bucket or simple spigot or just gravity. Continuous water flow almost certainly would not have been used. It would have been an undue burden on the Ark and its available resources, among which water would have been among the most critical. The collection portion of the toilet area could have been made of metal or earthenware[4] or some form of waterproofed wood. Alternatively, even more simply, waste could have landed in a smaller vessel on a small cart for removal to a designated collection area.

The solutions needed for human waste on board this immense ship is dwarfed by the daily waste output of the various animals. So, what would have been some very simple methods to manage this huge task?

Animal Waste

The Ark Encounter designs show Noah's family using carts and small wagons to move the solid animal waste. While this sounds like a lot of work, it would have been manageable. Some manual cleaning would be expected even with solutions built into the cage or enclosure designs.

The design of the enclosures could have made the waste removal task much simpler. Sloped floors[5] or designs that incorporated slatted floors[6] that allowed waste to slip through could have been used.

The Ark Encounter features some cages with "a design of finely slotted bamboo floors that allow for waste to pass through, roll down a lower ramp, and is collected in a single trough at the base of grouped cages. The sloppy waste of most flying creatures could be collected in simple trays under their slotted cages . . . most large-animal cages [are designed] with flat and solid floors, since slotted floors can result in leg or foot injuries."[7]

Factory farming of today uses some of these simple techniques in caring for thousands of animals a day. Though it is important to remember that while a factory farm is designed for maximum production with often minimal animal comfort, the Ark was built on the concept of caring for animals sent to it by God that would represent a new start at the end of the Flood. Simple care and consistent techniques could prevent animals from dying due to disease caused by unsanitary conditions. The Ark Encounter team considered the use of bedding for the animals, but they deemed it would have been more troublesome than it was worth, and it was unnecessary for the year on board the Ark.

Liquid waste would move into the bamboo piping and away from the enclosures

An example of collection trays of solid waste from bird cages being emptied into a small cart to be taken to a collection point.

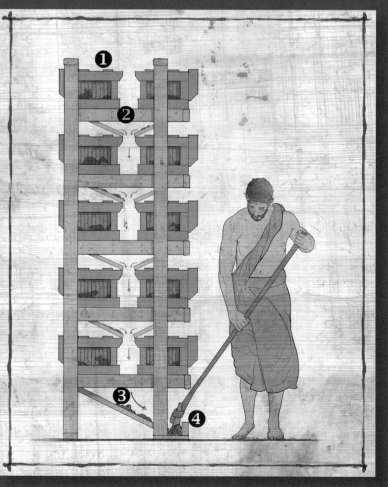

Simple cage designs become multifunctional when stacked so that ❶ waste falls from cage and is directed by a simple incline to ❷ an open center area, then ❸ an inclined collection point, from which ❹ waste can be gathered and transported to a central collection point.

Animal Transfer System

In the absence of bedding, each stall must eventually be cleaned out by hand. Regardless of animal diet or behavior, such confined spaces with large animals on a moving Ark was a genuinely dangerous proposition — in fact, the most dangerous creatures on the Ark may have been the large herbivores.

This led the Ark Encounter team to design the large animal enclosures with animal transfer systems. Each large animal cage has two doors: one that opens access to the aisle-way while simultaneously sealing off its end and another that opens into the cage from the side, isolating the animals in the aisle-way. Once the animals are isolated, cleaning can commence. Waste is then collected in carts and taken to the stern. The middle and upper decks of the stern feature a shaft where solid waste is dumped into a collection pit on the lower deck.[8]

Representative of the stahleckeriid kind modeled after *Placerias*

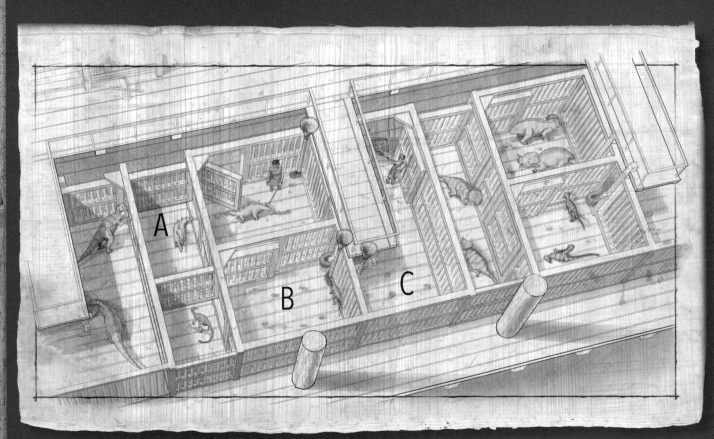

Large Animal Cage Transfer System: This allowed the family to clean out the cages safely. A) Doors are configured to help guide the animals to a small holding area within the pen safely. B) As a person entered the cage, the door would swing to close off the holding area. With cages side by side, the next cage would be accessed the same way. C) With the animals secured in the holding area, the cages could be safely and efficiently cleaned.

Solid waste removal on the Ark: ❶ waste is dropped down a shaft into ❷ a central collection point below, ❸ where an animal-powered, ❹ chain pump carries the waste up to ❺ a dispersal shaft, and is then released into one of the moon pools where the waste is released into the Flood waters.

A Hole in The Ship?

You may not yet be familiar with an important component that has been proposed as part of the Ark design. It's the concept of a moon pool.

"What is a moon pool? Well, picture a ship with a hole in the bottom of the hull and a wall surrounding the hole all the way up through the top deck — in the Ark's case, the roof. Water won't enter the ship because it's contained inside the moon pool's walls, moving up and down like a piston as the ship rides the waves."[9]

The Ark Encounter designers have placed two moon pools in the stern, straddling the keel. These moon pools are capped-off vertical shafts running the height of the Ark. These shafts are open at the bottom, permitting a relatively free flow of water within their interior. One moon-pool is used for ventilation, as the in-and-out movement of the water acts like a massive bellow, circulating air throughout the Ark.[10]

One moon pool is an integral part of the waste removal system on the Ark.

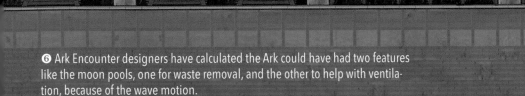

❻ Ark Encounter designers have calculated the Ark could have had two features like the moon pools, one for waste removal, and the other to help with ventilation, because of the wave motion.

Simple Automation

Dealing with large animal waste is an area of great concern. First, cleanup is often simplified when solid waste is separated from liquid waste. It is important to bear in mind that waste comes in all shapes, sizes, consistencies, and degrees of degradation. At the Ark Encounter, the flat floors in the large animal cages have a lip around them and a gutter that runs along the intersection of a cage grouping.[11] With this in place, movement of the ship would effectively separate the liquids from the solids.

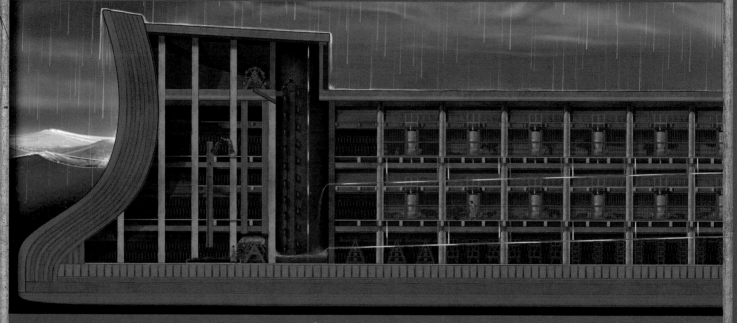

Liquid Waste Removal

Liquids then drain from the gutter into a pipe running nearly the length of the Ark and feed into a liquid waste collection tank. This tank would be located between two moon-pools in the stern — the back end — of the Ark.[12] The Ark Encounter's concept has the capacity to collect about a day's worth of liquid.

Inside this tank are two possible means of removing liquid waste. On most days, water would have risen and fallen within the moon pools. This movement could be exploited by designing a suction pipe with valves that runs from the base of the liquid waste collection track into the top of the waste moon pool. As waves lower in the waste moon pool, it creates suction in the pipe and pulls the liquid waste from the collection tank into the waste moon pool. As the waves and corresponding pressure rise in the waste moon pool, valves in the suction pipe close, permitting liquids to flow in only one direction. The Ark's occupants were obviously isolated during the Flood, so system redundancy was probably necessary. In the case of removing waste water, the Ark Encounter team also placed a chain pump inside the collection tank.

A chain pump is an ancient technology that uses human or animal power to efficiently pull liquids from one place and dump them in another. A wheel is located at the bottom of the collection tank, while another wheel is located at the top. Earthen buckets attached to a rope span from one wheel to the other like a belt between two pulleys. As one wheel is turned, the buckets are dipped into the waste and lifted to the top of the collection tank; as they lift over the top wheel, their contents are funneled down a chute into the waste moon pool. A system like this could be operated for several minutes at the end of each day or when conditions were insufficient for suction pumping.

Solid Waste Removal

These systems would work in concert with another simple device, the solid waste remover. This simple automation solution is not often seen in the developed world today because it is based on animal power.

The solid waste remover functions like the chain pump, dumping its contents into the waste moon pool and using the same drive system. The major difference between the two is that the larger buckets of the solid waste remover are loaded manually from a solid waste collection pit on the lower deck.

Power comes from an animal-driven treadmill, also on the lower deck. A single individual can simultaneously manage the animal and load the solid waste remover, thus massively conserving labor. All of these designs are simple mechanisms found in various cultures throughout history.

Dimensions of the proposed equipment limits its use and installation to the second and third decks. Distribution of the solid waste would occur as the waves recede from the port or starboard sides to keep splashback at a minimum. It could even have been an enclosed device to maximize unwanted contamination of areas in proximity to the system.

There are many animal-powered agricultural, industrial, waterworks, and mining applications found throughout history. These include oblique treadmills and even tread wheels. Other examples include one from the Ming Dynasty of water wheels driven by draught animals.[13] One scholar noted, "We have considerable knowledge of the use of animal-powered engines in prehistoric and classic times, but no certainty of their form until the Roman period."[14] The Amish regularly use animal treadmills, and the treadmill shown in the Ark Encounter waste removal video borrows a standard Amish design.

Representatives of the sloth kind modeled after *Hapalops*

45

Animal Waste — Just How Much?

An estimate was made that "[a]s much as 12 U.S. tons (11 m. tons) of animal waste may have been produced daily" on the Ark, though this number was formulated on the premise that there were 16,000 animals on board.[15]

Less than half that number of animals were aboard, and the average size of these animals was smaller than the estimates used in the study above, so the amount of waste produced daily on the Ark may have only been a few tons.

Close Proximity

While you may find it hard to imagine waste management with people and animals in such close proximity, it is important to remember that humans have lived close to their livestock since ancient times — both to protect the animals and to oversee their care. Life on the Ark would have been a natural extension of this and animal care standard practices seen throughout history:

"Archaeologists have excavated first century homes from the Judean hill country. They have discovered that the upper level served as a guest chamber while the lower level served as the living and dining rooms. Oftentimes, the more vulnerable animals would be brought in at night to protect them from the cold and theft. This sounds strange to many of us, since we wouldn't dream of bringing some of our cattle into the house at night, but even today in some countries of Europe (e.g., Germany and Austria), the farmhouse and the animal quarters are often different parts of the same building."[16]

Simple and Reliable

While one might consider reducing the amount of feed and water for the animal kinds so they would have used less water and produced less waste, the health and safety of the animals had to be the top concern. It would also take healthy, well-cared-for animals to reproduce after the Flood.[17] This means that proper care of them was the primary task for Noah and his family. Design features of the Ark helped to maximize usage of space, as well as minimize physical labor, but these systems did not need to be complex — merely reliable and functional.

"[The] history of the Indian civilization indicates that the people of Harappa in the Indus Valley had many toys that could move their heads and duplicate motions of wild animals. . . . there is enough indication that the early people discovered certain principles and knew simple mechanisms to create those wonders. Later the Chinese, Greek, and Roman civilizations designed and constructed many devices which were similar to the present-day machines and robots. . . . From these ideas, models, and mechanisms, grew the concept of early mechanization."[18]

Once again, when we take into account a biblical timeline rather than the secular dating — and historical details like Greek automata, Roman "robotics," and ancient Chinese technology — it shows ancient man was both intelligent and inventive.

Is This How Noah Actually Did It?

What you see at the Ark Encounter is a series of ideas about how Noah could have built the boat and successfully cared for the animal kinds. Unless the ancient vessel is ever found, what we know about Noah is given to us in few details in the Bible.

Chapter 7
Maintaining the Ark's Environment

"There are all sorts of possibilities. How about a plumbing system for gravity-fed drinking water, a ventilation system driven by wind or wave motion, or hoppers that dispense grain as the animals eat it? None of these require higher technology than what we know existed in ancient cultures."

— *The New Answers Book, Vol. 1*[1]

I t is easy to let your imagination wander when it comes to the possibilities of how the Ark worked. However, it is always important to come back to what we know, what might have worked, and how many animals may have been on board. The point of the ship was to save not just eight members of one family, which would have certainly been easier. Noah's task also included the care of at least two representatives of every land-dwelling representative of the animal kinds the Lord brought to him.

The gathering and storage of food as well as the water and waste systems have been discussed, but there is much more to be explored and considered when it comes to animal care. Could Noah's family properly ventilate and light the Ark? How could they care for animals that might get injured? Could they repair systems that might break down during the Flood?

Light Source Solutions

While not as noticeable as other solutions, lighting plays a key role in life on the Ark. Whether providing an energy source for plants to grow or making it easier to complete the chores needed in the depths of the ship, it was essential that methods be found for all the lighting needs on the ship – including hallways, living quarters, storage areas, animal areas, etc.

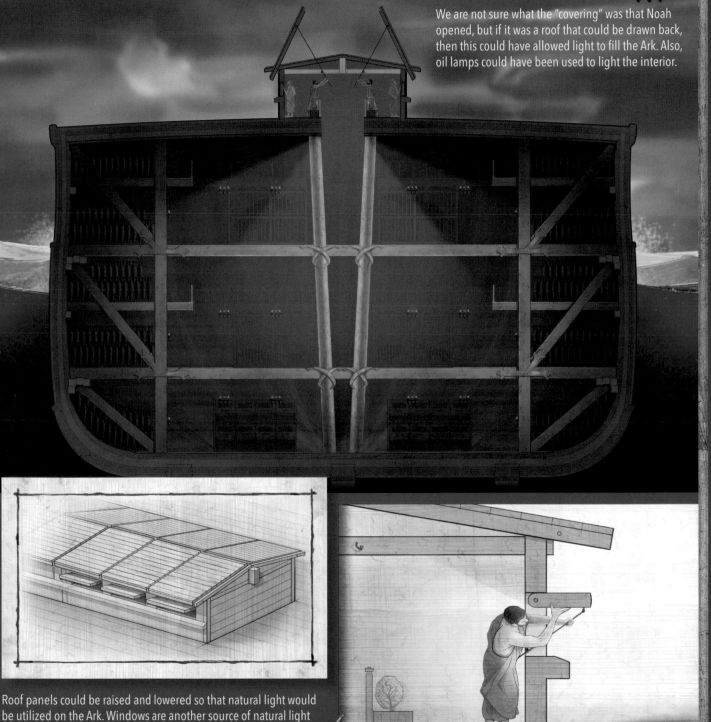

We are not sure what the "covering" was that Noah opened, but if it was a roof that could be drawn back, then this could have allowed light to fill the Ark. Also, oil lamps could have been used to light the interior.

Roof panels could be raised and lowered so that natural light would be utilized on the Ark. Windows are another source of natural light and could be part of a strategy to grow food.

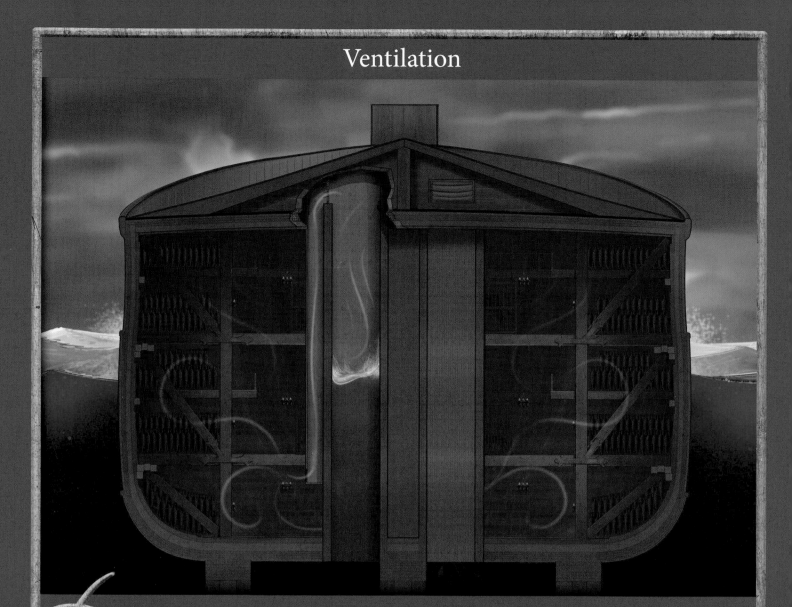

It was important for more than just sanitary reasons that the waste was removed. While not a concern that many people realize, researchers have even explored the potential danger of an explosion or toxic fumes from all of the waste. Woodmorappe writes,

"The danger of toxic or explosive manure gases, such as methane, would be alleviated by the constant movement of the Ark, which would have allowed manure gases to be constantly released. Second, methane, which is half the density of air, would quickly find its way out of a small opening such as window [in the Ark]. There is no reason to believe that the levels of these gases within the Ark would have approached hazardous levels. . . . While the voyage of the ark may not have been comfortable or easy, it was certainly doable, even under such unprecedented circumstances."[2]

The Ark Encounter team also used the moon pool concept to show how fresh air could have been circulated throughout the Ark by using the power of waves. The ventilation moon pool would be built adjacent to the waste moon pool in the stern of the Ark.

Representatives of the silesaur kind modeled after *Silesaurus*

Wave-Powered Purifier: Moon pools are generally used for drilling and research vessels, but the same concept could be applied to exploit the waves to pump air throughout the ark. It may seem strange to include a shaft or well inside the Ark that opens to the water below, but a moon pool would be an extremely effective mechanism to provide a continual supply of fresh air. ❶ Falling waves inside the moon pool pull in fresh air. ❷ Rising waves push the fresh air through the shaft to the bottom deck. ❸ Fresh air is directed into the lower level, ultimately bringing air to the other decks.

Chapter 8

Ancient Man: The Pre-Flood World

"St. Peter says that the whole world at that time perished by a great cataclysm of water. Our belief that the entire world was destroyed in the Flood is based especially on [2] Peter 3:6, where it says the "kosmos," the whole world that then was, was "cataclysmed" (Greek "kataklusmos") with water and perished. The entire structure, the entire system that then was, perished."

— Dr. Henry M. Morris[1]

Noah's Ark is a very interesting clue about the technology of the the antediluvian, or pre-Flood, world of mankind. The ship itself represents a wonderful mastery of materials and simple, effective technology, as well as a functional understanding of shipbuilding and animal care. But it also runs completely contrary to the secular dating scale and its assumptions about the development of man. The problems lie in three areas: origins, timescale, and evolution.

The Starting Point Matters

In the secular humanist worldview, ancient man evolves from ape-like ancestors over millions of years before being able to create the more-sophisticated-than-expected civilizations[2] still being unlocked today. But consider the biblical starting point. The God of all creation forms a world, animals, universe, two people, and countless wonders in the span of six normal-length days. Adam and Eve were created fully human and given stewardship over the world. They would also break the only prohibition God had placed on them by eating the fruit from the tree of knowledge of good and evil, which resulted in the Fall of Man.[3] Sin would only be compounded as Adam and Eve and their descendants populated the earth. It finally reached a point where God passed His judgment on His corrupted creation — it

would all be destroyed except for a righteous man named Noah, his family, and representatives of the animal kinds so that mankind could start again following the Flood's purge of the world.

But the Flood also represents the biggest challenge in understanding the pre-Flood world. By its nature and purpose — that of judgment on a wicked world — it destroyed the world that Noah knew. The Flood itself left us clues about the geological changes it wrought, as well as the devastation to the animals and vegetation. The lack of human fossils or pre-Flood civilization sites is likely due to the progression and catastrophic nature of the event.[4]

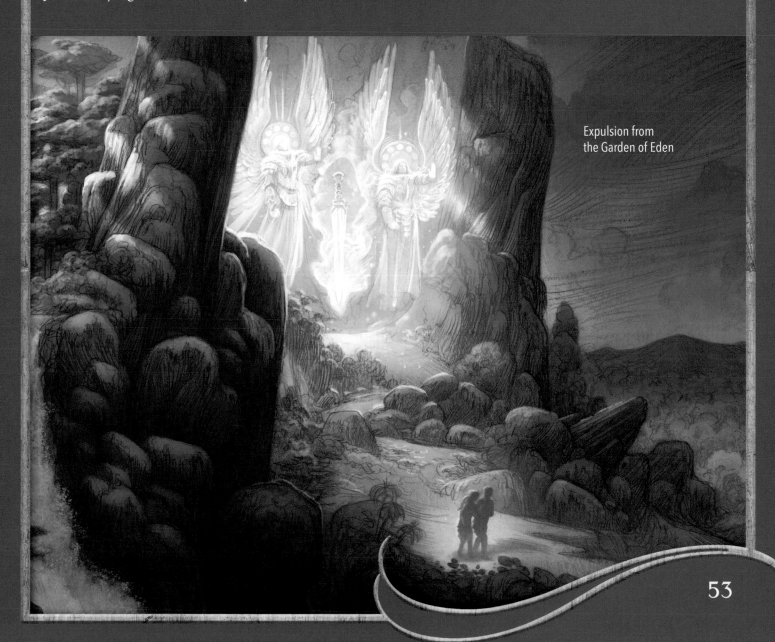

Expulsion from
the Garden of Eden

Biblical Clues

What can we glean from the biblical text about Noah's world? Details include:

- Mankind had mastered metalworking and music[5]
- Existence of four named rivers, lands, and natural resources[6]
- Wide variety of plants and animals — including dinosaurs
- Cycle of light and darkness in the form of days
- People ate, drank, and married[7]
- People became exceedingly wicked[8]
- There was no rain prior to the creation of man, but contrary to a popular belief, it probably did rain before the Flood.[9]

The use of music and metal shows that people of Noah's day were technologically advanced. The musical instruments could have been used for religious or entertainment purposes, which runs counter to evolutionary teaching about early man. Though wicked, the people of Noah's day were highly skilled and intelligent, having been made in the image of God. As mentioned earlier in this book, as far as we know, God gave Noah sparse instructions on the construction of the Ark. Scripture makes no mention of any divine intervention to assist Noah in the Ark's construction. There are no verses detailing angelic hosts helping out, or God, who created everything from nothing, suddenly just causing a boat to pop into existence. A straightforward reading of the biblical text is that Noah had the skills to build it[10] — God merely gave him the specifications of wood type, size, number of decks, need for pitch, an opening[11] at the top, and a door in its side.

That leaves a lot of blanks for Noah to fill in. While some civilizations never develop an alphabet or form of writing of their own, it can also be assumed that Noah's world also had some form of communication as a way of transmitting or preserving information. The Ark was not a product of random and desperate trial, error, and chance, but a product that took particular skills, experience, and engineering to create. It had to work. There was no Plan B.

Also note that God didn't send Noah on an animal scavenger hunt — God chose those Himself. He allowed Noah to have the time for the job to be completed. Hebrews 11:7 tells us that Noah "moved with godly fear" when he built the ark for the saving of his household.[12] This does not necessarily mean that he worked really fast, but that he took great care in what he was doing, building with great reverence.

Even the choice of a Flood is an interesting form of judgment. God had the power to destroy and refashion the world any way He wished — as evidenced in the promise to not use water again but fire the next time. God is God over all things. He had a lot of options. He chose a man — Noah, a means of safety — the Ark, and a method of judgment — the Flood. One intriguing question is just how much of the means and method was tied to the experiences and skills of the man?

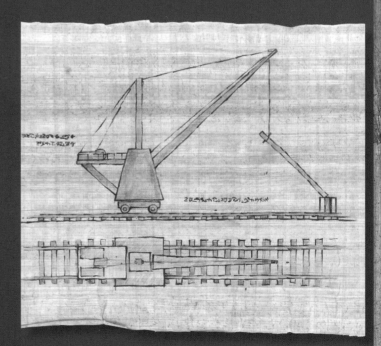

Plans for a simple crane that could have been moved along a simple rail system.

A Functional Floor Plan

Cross-section of the Ark, among Noah's documents at the Ark Encounter

With these clues in mind, what does this tell us? Noah was intelligent — he was smart enough to realize that he had huge issues to deal with beyond merely building the Ark. Surviving the Flood was just the first in a series of challenges. How would he and his family live once the floodwaters receded? They would need reliable shelter from the elements, food sources, and more importantly, the ability to reproduce the skills and technologies of the world that would be destroyed. Temporary housing could possibly be found in the Ark, water would be available, and there may have been enough food stores to draw from until seeds could be planted and harvested.

With a shape designed to help the ship survive the forces of the Flood, the Ark's interior design would have been just as carefully considered in order to maximize space for the animals, the family's living quarters, storage, gardens, and other needs.

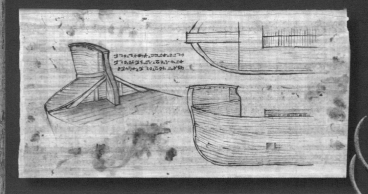

Japheth's wife paints in their room on the Ark at the Ark Encounter.

Room Design

If you consider a dual use of the Ark as post-Flood housing or even a source of future building materials, then it would only make sense that the rooms the family would live in for a year and beyond would be somewhat comfortable. Remember, God gave Noah the time to fashion the Ark — this was not necessarily a rush job. So you see this consideration in the Ark Encounter rooms that reveal the high level of finishing and craftsmanship for each. Inclusion of areas in the Ark devoted to gardens, weaving, woodworking, and blacksmithing represent other known skills needed during and after the journey.

The third deck of the Ark Encounter showcases living quarters for Noah and his family during the journey. These will also show unique features that differentiate the interests of the family members.[13] Many are recognizable as features you would find in simple housing today — sleeping quarters, a kitchen,[14] pantry, gardens, and dining area.[15]

Food supplies could have included a variety of preserved foods, wheats, grains, nuts, and possibly some fresh produce grown in the garden.[16] This would not have included meats for the people, but they may have made such provisions for some of the animals.[17]

In Genesis 1:29, Adam and Eve were commanded to eat "every herb that yields seeds . . . and every tree whose fruit yields seed," and it is not until after the Flood event that God gives man permission to eat animals, when "every moving thing that lives shall be food for you. I have given you all things, even as the green herbs" (Genesis 9:3).[18] It is logical to assume that Noah, noted for his obedience and righteousness, continued to obey the biblical prohibition against meat eating until God allowed it.

Among the staples of water and food storage, functional workshops, and comfortable living quarters in the Ark Encounter designs, you will also see what some may consider an unusual room — Noah's library.

Noah's Library would have preserved vital information for the world that would have to begin again.

Knowledge Preserved

We can see through cave art and early artifacts that knowledge and cultural information could be transmitted in a variety of ways, but it is important to concentrate on large-scale documentation efforts. If you go back to the earliest-known civilizations, such as the Sumerian culture,[19] you find methods of recordkeeping — either in temples or the records of ancient kings. The Library of Ashurbanipal is just one example.[20]

Ancient Egyptians also attempted to preserve knowledge,[21] and in some cases attempted to organize and catalog collections for easier use. Antiquity's greatest and most famous library was the Royal Library of Alexandria, which, sadly, was burned down, resulting in the total loss of perhaps hundreds of thousands of scrolls. There are numerous examples of ancient scholarship and ideas being "re-discovered" at later periods in time and clues for greater works discovered in citations of surviving documents.

Clearly some of the ancient cultures valued knowledge and learning, and the libraries served these important purposes. Yet, despite longevity beyond our dreams and divine favor, Noah

could not have mentally retained the sum of human knowledge at the time. Without any form of preserving this knowledge, it would be lost with the unexpected death of Noah or the others. Memories can fade. Knowledge not applied can be overlooked and forgotten. While there are probably many things from the wicked pre-Flood world Noah would have wanted to forget, it makes sense that Noah would have collected certain information for immediate and future use.

"According to the early chapters of Genesis, the pre-Flood period saw great leaps in technological advancement, meaning it is quite possible that people pioneered writing as well. . . . [In] Noah's library, you can see a large number of scrolls. These might have included information that Noah wanted to preserve from the pre-Flood culture such as notes about science, family records, and animals. In the Ark design studio, these clay tablets were fabricated for Noah's library."[22]

A sample of "Noah's language" from the Ark Encounter

Noah's Alphabet

In the display of Noah's library at the Ark Encounter, you will also see clay tablets with "Noah's language" written on them. Nothing is known about the language or writing used in Noah's time. Although the earliest forms of writing found have been pictorial in nature, the Ark Encounter team of researchers and designers have developed an alphabetic script to enhance the guest experience.

". . . on the Ark some of the exhibits will be written in what the team calls "Noah's language." It's a completely made up language and alphabet that looks like what we imagine Noah's language could have looked like written down. It's a font that's written right to left like Hebrew or Arabic, but it contains 26 letters and 10 numerals like English. This is so that a researcher can write out what the text would say in English and a designer can "translate" it to Noah's language when they complete the artwork."[23]

At the beginning of this book, we discussed Athanasius Kircher's attempt to show the layout of Noah's Ark. In his work, *Turris Babel*, he sought to understand the confusion of languages at the Tower of Babel and, as part of that, the original language of Adam and Eve. This language is referred to by some as the Adamic language or the Edenic language, and it would have been the pre-Flood language. In Kircher's time, like today, some people considered Hebrew to be the original language, and the confusion at Babel created other languages.

"From this starting point, Kircher took a philological approach, considering many languages and seeking to understand their relationship to one another. In effect the great work was almost a universal history of language: its goal was to explain how languages had multiplied and spread since Babel."[24] However, neither Kircher nor scholars today can definitively say what the original language may have been.

The Bible tells us in Genesis 10:31 of the nations that descended from the sons of Noah "according to their families, according to their languages, in their lands, according to their nations." This is generally understood to be the result of events after the dispersion of people groups from Babel. Genesis 11:1 notes that at Babel "the whole earth had one language and one speech,"[25] but what that language was cannot be known with certainty.

Specialized Skills

Weaving, blacksmithing, and woodworking are among the exhibits at the Ark Encounter. Evidence of weaving was been found at one of the earliest civilizations, Çatalhöyük, in Anatolia. Drawings of weavers in ancient Egypt have been found, as well as evidence of woven textiles in native tribes of the American Southwest, South America, Asia, India, and China.[26] The technique is not limited to clothing — it has also been used to make baskets, ornamentations, and a variety of other useful items.

Secular science has divided the history of mankind into "ages" based on the materials they mastered — the stone age, bronze age, iron age, copper age, and so on. But rather than needing to evolve for thousands of years to acquire the know-how, the Bible mentions metalworking seven generations after Adam. It is first mentioned in Genesis 4:20–22, which notes the births of Lamech's sons Jubal, "the father of all those who play the harp and flute," and Tubal-Cain, "an instructor of every craftsman in bronze and iron." The skill would have been essential both for making and repairing metal tools or components used on the Ark and for life after the Flood when they would leave the ship and make their new homes.

Wood is among the earliest mediums that man used to create functional tools or artistic pieces. Examples can be found among the earliest civilizations of Egypt, Greece, Rome, and China. Examples include beautiful furniture, even with veneers.[27] Archaeologists are just beginning to understand the art of shipbuilding in Ancient Egypt, but examples like the Khufu ship show their sophistication. The 1,224 different pieces[28] took researchers years to reassemble using the markings left for that purpose by the ancient craftsmen who carved it. The Ark was also a masterful example of woodworking taken to an extreme in terms of size, strength, and importance.

Conclusion

"I set My rainbow in the cloud, and it shall be for the sign of the covenant between Me and the earth."

— Genesis 9:13

As we have explored Noah's world and why his vessel with simple systems would have worked, we have to remember we look back at the work of God through perspectives influenced by a lost and fallen world. We too often want to relegate Noah to a cardboard Hollywood hero or the Flood to myth or allegorical fiction. We look around at our world of advanced technology and assume our knowledge and understanding of the world surpasses any other age. Yet, we are reminded again in mysterious ruins and cryptic glimpses of ancient glory, such as Stonehenge and the Great Pyramid, that the story of mankind is not one of evolution but one of created beings with unimaginable potential to unlock the secrets of the world God created for us.

It's easy to say Noah's Ark is just a morality tale for children or a metaphor for an angry God who will punish disobedience and sin. But the uncomfortable reality is Noah was simply a man — a man of faith, a man of obedience, yet also a man with flaws. In four short biblical chapters, Noah goes from a man whose birth was one that would "comfort" and his life would find "grace in the eyes of God" to one who became drunk and passed out. Noah wasn't a perfect man, but he was a righteous one.

Noah as a man may have had an amazing skill set and vast amounts of knowledge per his longevity, but he is not all that different from us today. When given a mission by God, he faithfully implemented and completed it using the abilities and techniques and materials he had available to him. The viability and reality of the Ark in the historical record are disturbing to many skeptics because it leads to an inevitable conclusion. The Bible has given us an accurate account of history.

Sin corrupted the created world, and God chose to destroy it. He picked one family and representatives of the land-dwelling animal kinds to be saved and start the world anew. There are consequences to sin and disobedience. Our relationship with God will determine our future as it did for Noah, his family, and, tragically, all those lost in the Flood.

As sinners, there will be consequences for us as well, but we can be saved by making the choice to receive Jesus Christ, our Savior, as revealed in the Bible.

And the bow shall be in the cloud; and I will look upon it, that I may remember the everlasting covenant between God and every living creature of all flesh that is upon the earth. And God said unto Noah, This is the token of the covenant, which I have established between me and all flesh that is upon the earth.

— Genesis 9:16-17

The Rainbow Covenant

End Notes

Introduction

1   "The 60 Minutes/Vanity Fair Poll," Vanity Fair, January 2010, http://www.vanityfair.com/magazine/2010/01/60-minutes-poll-201001?currentPage=2.

Chapter 1:

1   Dr. Tommy Mitchell, "There Was No Rain Before the Flood," Answers in Genesis, October 19, 2010, https://answersingenesis.org/creationism/arguments-to-avoid/there-was-no-rain-before-the-flood/.

2   Ark Encounter, "How Long Is a Cubit," Answers in Genesis, accessed September 22, 2016, https://arkencounter.com/noahs-ark/cubit/. [The cubit varied in length per culture. See Answers in Genesis, "Putting the Ark into Perspective," Answers in Genesis, January 23, 2014, https://answersingenesis.org/noahs-ark/putting-the-ark-into-perspective/. The Ark Encounter uses the Nippur cubit at 20.4 inches, equating to just over 1.70 feet per cubit.]

3   Details from the New King James Version (NKJV) of Genesis 6:14–16.

Chapter 2:

1   Dr. Henry Morris, The Henry Morris Study Bible, commentary notes on Genesis 6:15 (Green Forest, AR: Master Books, 2012), p. 34-35.

2   Augustine, The City of God, Book 15, Chapter 27, "Of the Ark and the Deluge, and that We Cannot Agree with Those Who Receive the Bare History, But Reject the Allegorical Interpretation, Nor with Those Who Maintain the Figurative and Not the Historical Meaning" (Buffalo, NY: Christian Literature Publishing, Co. 1887), accessed September 22, 2016, http://www.newadvent.org/fathers/120115.htm.

3   Augustine, The City of God, Book 15, Chapter 27, "Of the Ark and the Deluge, and that We Cannot Agree with Those Who Receive the Bare History, But Reject the Allegorical Interpretation, Nor with Those Who Maintain the Figurative and Not the Historical Meaning" accessed September 22, 2016, http://www.episcopalnet.org/READINGS/CityOfGod/Bk15/Ch27.html.

4   Origen, Homilies on Genesis and Exodus, Ronald E. Heine, translator (Washington, DC: CUA Press, 2010), p. 73.

5   Ibid., 73-74.

6   Celsus, On the True Doctrine: A Discourse Against the Christians, translated by R. Joseph Hoffman (New York: Oxford University Press, 1987), p. 80.

7   Flavius Josephus, Josephus: The Complete Works, Chapter 3, accessed September 22, 2016, http://www.ccel.org/ccel/josephus/complete.ii.ii.iii.html.

8   Colin Schutz, "How One 17th Century Scholar Reconciled Newly Discovered Species and the Space on Noah's Ark" Smithsonian Magazine, October 28, 2013, http://www.smithsonianmag.com/smart-news/how-one-17th-century-scholar-reconciled-newly-discovered-species-and-the-space-on-noahs-ark-5936603.

9   Paula Findlen, Possessing Nature: Museums, Collecting, and Scientific Culture in Early Modern Italy (Berkeley, CA: University of California Press, 1994), p. 91-92.

10   Olaf Breidbach and Michael T. Ghiselin, "Athanasius Kircher (1602–1680) on Noah's Ark: Baroque 'Intelligent Design' Theory," Proceedings of the California Academy of Sciences, Fourth Series, vol. 57, no. 36, http://researcharchive.calacademy.org/research/scipubs/pdfs/v57/proc-cas_v57_n36.pdf, p. 992.

11   Morris, The Henry Morris Study Bible, commentary notes on Genesis 6:16, p. 35.

12   John Woodmorappe, Noah's Ark: A Feasibility Study (El Cajon, CA: Institute for Creation Research, 2003) p. xi.

13   Tim Lovett, Noah's Ark: Thinking Outside the Box (Green Forest, AR: Master Books, 2008), p. 45.

14   Larry Pierce, "The Large Ships of Antiquity," Creation Ministries International, accessed September 22, 2016, http://creation.com/the-large-ships-of-antiquity.

15   Maya Wei-Haas, "Antikythera Shipwreck Yields New Cache of Ancient Treasures," Smithsonian Magazine, September 29, 2015, http://www.smithsonianmag.com/science-nature/antikythera-shipwreck-yields-new-cache-ancient-treasures-180956775/.

16   Tim Lovett, "Feedback: Are Wooden Ships Reliable? Part 2," Answers in Genesis, June 14, 2013, https://answersingenesis.org/noahs-ark feedback-are-wooden-ships-reliable/.

Chapter 3:

1   Tim Lovett, "Thinking Outside the Box," Answers in Genesis, March 19, 2007, https://answersingenesis.org/noahs-ark/thinking-outside-the-box/.

2   The Ark Encounter research indicates that if just the basic dimensions were taken and multiplied, it would be 2.21 million, but 15 percent of the square footage per deck is lost because of the curve of the ship's design. By adjusting the square footage and multiplying by the height, the result would be 1.88 million cubic feet.

3   Dr. Jean Lightner et al., "Determining the Ark Kinds," Answers in Genesis, November 16, 2011, https://answersingenesis.org/noahs-ark/determining-the-ark-kinds/.

4   Ark Encounter, "How Many Animals Were on Noah's Ark?", Answers in Genesis, accessed September 23, 2016, https://arkencounter.com/animals/how-many/.

5   According to the Ark Encounter design team, "as for the number fabricated for Ark Encounter, however, [note] that cage number, placement, and design are areas where our hypothetical model of Noah's Ark differ from the Troyer Ark."

Chapter 4:

1   Ark Encounter Blog, "Noah's Floating Farm of Animals and Plants," August 31, 2012, https://arkencounter.com/blog/2012/08/31/noahs-floating-farm-of-animals-and-plants/

2   Dr. Georgia Purdom, "No Taste for Meat?" March 30, 2009, https://answersingenesis.org/animal-behavior/what-animals-eat/no-taste-for-meat/

3   Woodmorappe, Noah's Ark: A Feasibility Study, p. 20. The author's calculation for the ark's total volume was at 43,169 cubic meters. He also writes "I assume, for purposes of calculation only, that no suspended animation of any kind ever took place among the animals on the Ark." Woodmorappe, Noah's Ark: A Feasibility Study, p. 17.

4   Hypothetically, a series of cisterns with a dispersion system could suffice for all human and animal needs. A water-collection system connected to the cisterns would mean that less water would need to be stored on the ark at any given time.

5   The surface area of the ark's roof was used by the Ark Encounter Team to determine how much water could be collected if the water that fell on the roof was collected in cisterns. The calculation included the premise that rain continued to fall during the Flood. One inch per week would have been easily attainable during the Flood. With the warmer ocean temperatures due to the volcanoes, geysers, etc. at the outset of the Flood, there would have been much more evaporation, and hence, precipitation, than we have today.

6   The Ark Encounter team used the following calculation to determine water usage by the animals. Generally, (371 days — assuming water was needed to be stored for the entire 371 days) x (the number of animals in a given mass category) x (average water needs per animal in a given mass category) x (metabolic factor) x (juvenile factor applied to the highest mass categories, according to metabolism, since many of the animals may have been growing), equals the basic water needs for a given mass/metabolic category. Then each category was added together for the total basic water needs. After that, a contingency of 25 percent was included to complete the calculation. For example: the basic estimated water needs of one example of the animal kinds, an extant (1-10 Mg) mammal, is: $(371)(6)(140L)(1)(0.05\ JF)=15.582\ KL$.

7   "How Much Water Was On Board the Ark?", Answers in Genesis, April 13, 2015, https://answersingenesis.org/noahs-ark/how-much-water-was-on-board-the-ark/.

Chapter 5:

1   John Woodmorappe, "Caring for the Animals on the Ark," Answers in Genesis, March 29, 2007, https://answersingenesis.org/noahs-ark/caring-for-the-animals-on-the-ark/.

2   United Nations Environmental Programme, Division of Technology, Industry and Economics, Sourcebook of Alternative Technologies for Freshwater Augmentation in Some Countries in Asia, "3.12 Bamboo Pipe Water Supply System," accessed September 22, 2016, http://www.unep.or.jp/ietc/publications/techpublications/techpub-8e/bamboo.asp. The article also notes that bamboo will decay and have to be replaced each year. However, since the ark's journey was only slightly over a year, a bamboo piping system would have probably been able to last the duration of the Flood event.

3 Depending on the actual design, the railing around the catwalks that overhang the cages could be used as a fulcrum when pouring.

Chapter 6:

1 Charles H. Spurgeon, "Noah's Faith, Fear, Obedience, and Salvation," (sermon, Metropolitan Tabernacle, Newington, London, England, June 1, 1890), accessed September 23, 2016, http://www.spurgeon.org/sermons/2147.php.

2 It should also not be forgotten that God closed the ark door per Genesis 7:16: "So those that entered, male and female of all flesh, went in as God had commanded him; and the LORD shut him in." The only other reference to opening an access to the ark is Noah removing the ark's "covering" in Genesis 8:13.

3 Nate Barksdale, "Who invented the flush toilet?", History, May 19, 2015, http://www.history.com/news/ask-history/who-invented-the-flush-toilet; notes that some ancient examples that "utilized a constant stream of water to carry away waste date back at least 5,000 years." This dating is secular; considering a biblical timeline, the ingenuity of ancient man is still obvious.

4 Claire Sudduth, "A Brief History of Toilets" , Time, November 19, 2009, http://content.time.com/time/health/article/0,8599,1940525,00.html; the Palace of Knossos is noted to have used earthenware pans with water supplied by terracotta pipes.

5 Woodmorappe, *Noah's Ark: A Feasibility Study*, p. 26. He notes "It is not at all difficult to visualize Noah having been familiar with sloped floors, as their origins clearly go back into antiquity. For instance, a Late Bronze Age livestock shed, discovered in England, possesses a sloping floor which empties into a central manure tank ([R.] Trow-Smith 1957, [*A History of British Livestock Husbandry to 1700* (London: Routledge and Kegan Paul),] p. 25–6.")) He goes on to suggest vermicomposting, a process using worms to break down waste into a compost.

6 Ibid., p. 27. He explains "It would have taken little imagination to notice that animals could stand on such boards so that their urine runs through and, then, as suggested by Baxter ([S.H. Baxter, *Intensive Pig Production*, London: Granada,]1984a, p. 258.) someone would note that, with appropriately sized and spaced holes in the boards, the animals would also trample their manure through the board into the pit below."

7 Notes from the Ark Encounter team.

8 Notes from the Ark Encounter team.

9 Answers in Genesis, "What's a Moonpool?", Answers in Genesis, November 22, 2013, https://answersingenesis.org/noahs-ark/whats-a-moonpool/; "Although the concept has been around a long time, it wasn't used much until recently with the arrival of drill ships designed for oil exploration. . . . Why may Noah have put a hole in his ship on purpose? There are several sound engineering reasons. First, a hole in the bottom of a long ship, as was the Ark, would help relieve hull stress as the vessel crested a wave. Second, the rising and falling water within the moonpool could be used to draw in fresh air and also extract stale air. Third, recent research has shown that moonpools induce resistance to movement. For Noah's ship, this may have dampened wave motion, making the voyage more tolerable for man and beast."

10 Notes from the Ark Encounter team.

11 Ibid.

12 Ibid.

13 Ian Inkster, *History of Technology, Vol. 25* (London: Bloomsbury Publishing, 2010), p. 164.

14 Ian McNeil, editor, *An Encyclopedia of the History of Technology* (London and New York: Routledge Reference, 2002), p. 262.

15 John Woodmorappe, "How Could Noah Fit the Animals on the Ark and Care for Them?" Answers in Genesis, October 15, 2013, https://answersingenesis.org/noahs-ark/how-could-noah-fit-the-animals-on-the-ark-and-care-for-them/.

16 Tim Chaffey, "Born in a Barn (Stable?)", Answers in Genesis, November 30, 2010, https://answersingenesis.org/holidays/christmas/born-in-a-barn-stable/.

17 This minimizes the potential risk that hungry animal kinds would have preyed on one another.

18 S.R. Deb and Sankha Deb, *Robotic Technology and Flexible Automation* (New Delhi: Tata McGraw-Hill Education, 2010), p. 2-3.

Chapter 7:

1 Ken Ham and Tim Lovett, , "Was There Really a Noah's Ark & Flood?", The New Answers Book 1ed. Ken Ham, (Green Forest, AR: Master Books, 2006), p. 130.

2 Woodmorappe, "Caring for the Animals on the Ark," https://answersingenesis.org/noahs-ark/caring-for-the-animals-on-the-ark/.

Chapter 8:

1 Dr. Henry M. Morris, "The Pre-Flood World," (lecture, Creation Seminar, Springfield, IL, July 8, 1968), http://www.creationmoments.com/content/pre-flood-world.

2 David B. Smith, "Overturning Expectations About Ancient Man," Answers in Genesis, April 1, 2014, https://answersingenesis.org/archaeology/ancient-technology/overturning-expectations-about-ancient-man/.

3 Also, notice in the biblical history that once they realized their naked state, they began to fashion clothing from vegetation in the Garden of Eden. This also is a clue that man had the ability to analyze problems, look around in his environment, and attempt to create solutions. But we see as the story continues that man cannot solve the biggest problem he has made — that of sin. Thus, God Himself must make them a new covering and ultimately send His Son to the Cross for mankind's salvation.

4 Dr. Morris notes: "It is significant that we find very few human fossils. The reason probably is that most men, representing the highest form of life, and the most mobile, would be able to reach the high hill before being caught by the Flood waters. After finally being overtaken and drowned, they would float on the surface and would only rarely be trapped and then buried in the sediments. Actually, the problem of the scarcity of human fossils is more serious for the evolutionist than for the creationist. If the earth were really billions of years old, and if man has actually lived several million years on earth, we ought to be able to find multitudes of prehistoric human fossils rather than only few widely scattered bone fragments. Especially should we find many fossils of primates evolving from animal life to modern man, but instead have found no such half-way creatures at all," Morris, "The Pre-Flood World," http://www.creationmoments.com.

com/content/pre-flood-world.

5 Genesis 4:19–22.

6 "Now a river went out of Eden to water the garden, and from there it parted and became four riverheads. The name of the first is Pishon; it is the one which skirts the whole land of Havilah, where there is gold. And the gold of that land is good. Bdellium and the onyx stone are there. The name of the second river is Gihon; it is the one which goes around the whole land of Cush. The name of the third river is Hiddekel [or Tigris]; it is the one which goes toward the east of Assyria. The fourth river is the Euphrates (Genesis 2:10–14).

7 Luke 17:27.

8 Genesis 6:5–6, 11–13.

9 This discussion is centered around Genesis 2:5–6: "before any plant of the field was in the earth and before any herb of the field had grown. For the LORD God had not caused it to rain on the earth, and there was no man to till the ground; but a mist went up from the earth and watered the whole face of the ground." Though often applied by some to have been this way up to the events of the Great Flood, the Bible does not indicate one way or another. There is also the question of rain as part of a natural water cycle after the creation week. Mitchell, " There Was No Rain Before The Flood," https://answersingenesis.org/creationism/arguments-to-avoid/there-was-no-rain-before-the-flood/.

10 Hebrews 11:7.

11 Although commonly referred to as a window today, it may not be that simple. "Most Bibles make some unusual translation choices for certain key words. Elsewhere in the Bible, the Hebrew word translated here as 'rooms' is usually rendered 'nests'; 'pitch' would normally be called 'covering'; and 'window' would be 'noon light.' Using these more typical meanings, the Ark would be something like this: The tebah (ark) was made from gopher wood, it had nests inside, and it was covered with a pitch-like substance inside and out. It was 300 cubits long, 50 cubits wide, and 30 cubits high. It had a noon light that ended a cubit upward and above, it had a door in the side, and there were three decks." Bodie Hodge and Tim Lovett, "What Did Noah's Ark Look Like?", September 3, 2013, Answers in Genesis, https://answersingenesis.org/noahs-ark/what-did-noahs-ark-look-like/.

12 Some consider Noah as having been an active evangelist, urging people to turn away from their wickedness, during the construction of the ark. Genesis 6:18 states "But I will establish My covenant with you; and you shall go into the ark — you, your sons, your wife, and your sons' wives with you." Ark Encounters, "Noah in the Bible," Answers in Genesis, accessed September 23, 2016, https://arkencounter.com/noah/.

13 Hodge and Lovett, "What Did Noah's Ark Look Like?", https://arkencounter.com/blog/2016/03/28/assembling-noahs-living-quarters/.

14 Not much is known about on-board food preparation on the oldest of ancient vessels. Artifacts found on the Kyrenia shipwreck included cookware. "Apparently these were used in cooking crew food ashore, in the manner suggested by Homer's Odyssey." Simon Spalding, *Food at*